Homeless – But for St Mungo's

Homeless – But for St Mungo's

George Tremlett

UNWIN

HYMAN

LONDON SYDNEY WELLINGTON

First published in Great Britain by the Trade Division of
Unwin Hyman Limited, 1989.

UNWIN HYMAN LIMITED
15–17 Broadwick Street
London W1V 1FP

Allen & Unwin Australia Ltd
8 Napier Street, North Sydney, NSW 2060, Australia

Allen & Unwin New Zealand Pty Ltd with the Port Nicholson Press
60 Cambridge Terrace, Wellington, New Zealand

British Library Cataloguing in Publication Data

Tremlett, George, *1939–*
    Homeless – but for St Mungo's.
1. London. Hostels for homeless single persons
I. Title
363.5'9

ISBN 0–04–440344–5

Set in 11 on 13 point Century Schoolbook by
Computape (Pickering) Limited, North Yorkshire
Printed in Great Britain at the
University Press, Cambridge

Introduction

It is not usual for a Socialist to be able to write an introduction to a book written by a Conservative on a subject of current bitter political controversy. It has been possible in this case not because I agree with George Tremlett's politics but because I accept his humanity as sincere. The book is largely a description of how things are. Between its covers you will find the stories of a few of the many people who are deprived of a home – something that most of us take for granted. Often, barely hanging on to a marginal existence at the edge of society, they leap from the page as larger than life characters. These are their stories and they have been put on paper by someone who himself fits into that larger than life category.

I first met George Tremlett shortly after my election to the Greater London Council in 1973, at a time when the new Labour administration had announced a major policy change on the treatment of homeless families. Previously, it had been left to the borough councils alone to tackle this problem, but with the wave of illegal evictions that followed the house price boom in the early 1970s they could no longer cope with the increasing tide of homelessness. Many of the newly elected members such as myself had been borough councillors and were determined that the new administration should use part of the GLC's vast housing resources to assist the boroughs in tackling this crisis, and we set out to change the previous policy. In the early radical days of that new administration, we rapidly overcame the opposition of those GLC officers who feared that homeless families, some of whom suffered from massive social problems arising from neglect by both central and local government, would 'lower the tone' of our estates and the new policy was pushed through at one of the earliest meetings of the new GLC.

The new policy was not supported by the Tory opposition and the debate was expected to be a heated one. After a couple of predictably reactionary speeches from the Tory benches, the Chair called George Tremlett. There was an immediate quickening of interest from old hands who had served on the Council previously and it was obvious to the new members that this must be one of the opposition's better speakers. We were not disappointed. By the time he had finished speaking George Tremlett had effectively cut the ground from under those who opposed the new policy more effectively than any of the Labour speakers could have done. He spoke movingly of the desperate plight he had known as a child during the housing crisis which followed the Second World War and the pain and anger he had felt at the insensitivity that previous Tory speakers had shown to the condition of the homeless. It was a memorable speech not just because it was the first act of rebellion in the new Council but because it was delivered by the best debater on the Tory benches.

Many of the new members such as myself made the initial mistake of assuming that Tremlett was on the left of his party. We only discovered later, and to our cost, that he was one of the new breed of populist, working-class Tories who were going to start cutting so deeply into the Labour vote when the Callaghan government began to disintegrate in the mid 1970s.

Tremlett was soon promoted to lead the GLC Tories on housing and seemed for a long time to be the heir apparent to Sir Horace Cutler, the Tory leader. However, his career in the GLC Tory group came to an unexpected and dramatic end in 1982 when he helped to uncover serious fraud in the accounts of a housing association which involved three of the most senior members of the Tory group. His refusal to take part in a cover-up and his decision to tell all he had been able to discover to the independent inquiry, which my Labour administration had established, made him an outcast in the Tory ranks. He also decided to take a vigorous part in the campaign to try to save the GLC from abolition by Mrs Thatcher's government, and this led to his expulsion from the Tory group at County Hall who found his repeated, public, savage and intellectual demolition of Thatcher's policy damaging to their chances of getting knighthoods as a reward for muting their criticism of abolition.

Muting criticism was not a characteristic that came naturally to George Tremlett, as I discovered in our frequent and often memorable clashes in the council chamber. But whatever ideological differences we had (and continue to have) there was never any question that he always retained his very sincere commitment to the homeless which was displayed in that first speech I heard him deliver back in 1973.

There was another larger than life character who stands out from the bland, grey figures who dominated that 1973 GLC administration and his name became synonymous with the crusade against homelessness – Paddy O'Connor – the tragic hero of this book.

In a milder version of the suspicious and poisonous atmosphere which greeted me when I arrived in Parliament fourteen years later, my election to the GLC was not a matter for universal rejoicing amongst Labour's old guard. Given that Paddy's job as Deputy Chief Whip was to maximise the Labour vote and minimise support for any rebellions, I did not expect that he would be someone whom I would come to treat as a friend and ally; but perhaps because he was himself a natural rebel we soon developed a close friendship. In one of our earliest conversations he confided that the reason behind my frosty welcome at County Hall was a warning GLC leaders had had from the leadership of Lambeth Council that I was a 'troublesome little bastard'. As he was constantly being obstructed by Lambeth Council over his plans to use the old Marmite factory to house the single homeless, he automatically assumed that I must be on the side of the angels in the rows that constantly split the Lambeth Labour Group. Working with him in his struggle to overcome Lambeth's objections to the use of the Marmite factory cemented our friendship, and I knew that whenever I was in trouble for breaking group discipline I could count on Paddy to be arguing within the whip's committee for me to be let off yet again.

His knowledge of the Irish republican movement and the history of Ireland was authoritative. More than anyone else, he taught me about Britain's role in Ireland and our long conversations in the members' reading room, as I picked his brains and listened to his advice, were decisive in the evolution of my own views on the issue. Years later when he knew he was dying, he told the organisers of the Troops Out Movement to 'rattle my bones in a good cause' and it was left to them and his family to organise a memorial meeting with the theme of Irish unity and freedom. I felt honoured to be the main speaker at that meeting (which the civic dignitaries who had flocked to attend his funeral managed to avoid).

In actual fact, as I came to know more about Paddy O'Connor's history, it became almost impossible to understand how he had ever been elected to the post of Deputy Whip except on the poacher turned gamekeeper principle. Exactly like the Liverpool and Lambeth councillors of today, he was surcharged and barred from holding office for five years when as a St Pancras borough councillor he refused to implement the Macmillan government's rent laws which he considered to be unjust. When he was eventually re-elected to the council he became the mayor and achieved an almost legendary status with his unorthodox approach to the mayoralty. His most famous escapade came when the council decided to crack down on rent arrears and eventually undertook their first eviction on one of the old St Pancras estates. Although a crowd of several hundred turned up to prevent the eviction, they

were no match for the police and council officers who
eventually managed to clear the crowds out of the way,
smash down the barricaded doors, throw the tenants and
their furniture on to the street, secure the flat and leave a
council officer on guard inside. As the defeated and demo-
ralised crowd was beginning to disperse the chauffeur-
driven, mayoral limousine drew up and out stepped
Paddy complete with mayoral chain and a vast sledge
hammer which took only one blow to smash open the door
to the flat. 'You can go back in now,' announced the
mayor to the delight of the tenants and the surprised
horror of the council officials and police who had no idea
whether the mayor had the power to do this or not. By the
time they discovered that he did not it was too late to do
anything about it and the council quietly dropped the
eviction policy.

It was that sort of approach which left no one in his
community in any doubt that Paddy was 'on our side – not
one of them'. It was little wonder that on the Sunday
before election day the priest of the parish announced to
the congregation: 'I have no right to tell you how to vote
next week but I just want you to know that I shall be
voting for Paddy O'Connor.'

When Paddy's world began to fall apart Tremlett
defended him from the charge of corruption, saying that
Paddy's problem was that he 'allowed his heart to rule his
head'. To which Paddy replied, 'What's a fucking heart
for?' That was the essence of his humanity and because it
could not be fitted into the media's neat little categories of
good and bad, it eventually killed him. Paddy O'Connor
was the first of my friends to be driven to an early grave
by the media in full hue and cry (and I doubt he will be
the last).

I can only imagine the pleasure and energy with which
Paddy would have thrown himself into the activities of
the radical socialist administration which was eventually
elected to run the GLC in 1981. But I know he would have

been a vocal supporter of the stand we took on Irish unity
and the memory of what the media had done to him only
made me more determined to resist them when they tried
to destroy me in the same way.

George Tremlett talks in this book of the changes in
attitudes and policies towards the homeless that came
about because of Paddy's crusade, but there were other
consequences of his impact on the 'correct way of doing
things'. When the new Labour administration took office
in 1981 and set out to follow Paddy's example of working
with, and funding some of, the less orthodox groups in the
voluntary sector, we built in strong checks and controls to
ensure that that trust was not abused. Although it was, of
course, too late to help Paddy, we had learnt from his
mistakes and out of all the many thousands of groups we
funded none of them landed us in the sort of mess which
had destroyed him.

Paddy O'Connor helped to change the way we view the
single homeless and in his conclusions George Tremlett
agrees with Paddy's belief that you can only help the
single homeless on their own terms. For many that is the
only right they have left and they would rather reject
help than surrender it.

Reading this book as a Socialist there is a further
conclusion I would draw, as Paddy himself would have
done. The single homeless are at the bottom of society's
pile and anything that worsens the conditions further up
will have a disproportionate affect at the bottom. The
lunatic house price boom has made it more and more
difficult for anyone who does not already own a home to
get their feet on the first rung of the housing ladder. At
the same time, the Thatcher government has made its
greatest cut of all in the field of council housing. Twenty
years ago the government of the day built nearly a
quarter of a million homes for rent a year. When this
government first took office ten years ago it inherited a
rented housing programme which still provided around

150,000 new homes a year. Now, it is barely a tenth of that. In London, with all its problems of homelessness, its squalid little bed and breakfast 'hotels' and rapidly decaying housing stock, the government has cut the council housing programme from the 25,000 a year it inherited to just 2,000 a year.

The consequences of this government's policy are appalling. Britain is the sixth richest nation in the world and yet people of all ages sleep and die on the streets of its capital city. The government, in order to save money for further tax cuts for the rich and its ever increasing arms programme, has announced a policy of 'community care', is closing its old Victorian mental homes, throwing their inhabitants on to the streets to live or die as best they can. There is a particular irony in this for a government which prides itself on its Victorian values, for it was the Victorians that first built the great old mental hospitals in order to get the casualties of the Industrial Revolution off the streets. A century later, this government of latter day Victorians is throwing them back on to the streets in order to cut public spending and sell off the profitable development sites that remain when the old hospitals are demolished.

As the housing crisis worsens we see the explosion of house prices closing off the opportunity of home ownership and forcing ever larger numbers of people into competition for the declining pool of public and private rented accommodation. Faced with the government's restrictions on new house building, councils have been driven to force homeless families with young children into accepting unsatisfactory and often appalling old flats on semi-derelict estates or in high rise blocks. These are exactly the kinds of homes which councils had been making available to single people and childless couples before the present government's housing cuts started to bite.

In 1971, as the public swung decisively against the Heath government, Labour took control of many councils and a new generation of younger and more radical councillors were elected. It was only a few years after the stunning documentary 'Cathy Come Home' that Shelter was at the height of its influence and for most of the new councils the key issue was housing. In the best of those new administrations such as Camden and Islington, in London, the councillors had the determination and courage to expand massively the inadequate housing programmes they had inherited. Although many mistakes were made, the simple fact remains that by 1979 they had dealt with half the bad housing within their boundaries and it was possible to envisage the end of the housing problem by the late 1980s.

That hope was crushed when the new Thatcher government started vetoing the majority of new housing schemes and took new legislative powers to prevent any council spending any money from any source to build new, or modernise old, housing. That is why housing is falling into disrepair at an increasing rate whilst an army of families and young single people exist for years in the squalor of bed and breakfast. That is why hundreds of thousands of building workers have known years of unemployment whilst tens of thousands of all ages sleep on the streets, night after night.

Until a government is prepared to fund a major house-building programme again, the conditions George Tremlett describes will continue as an indictment of our whole society.

KEN LIVINGSTONE

Chapter 1

The last train leaves. The station shuts. There you are, with not enough money in your pocket to hire a taxi or book into a cheap hotel. Having left your credit cards at home, you start walking. It is a familiar mishap. Anyone can miss that last train home, but it's only when you do that you realise the railway authorities close their lavatories, too, and you may have to relieve yourself in a darkened doorway, or walk the streets for hours, searching for an all night coffee stall.

Only then, wandering alone in the night, do you find your normal world has vanished. The shutters are down. Shops and cafes have closed. Even the policemen never know where you might find a coffe stall. Finding one becomes important. You are cold and thirsty. It may be raining, which makes it worse. Slowly you realise that you are not alone after all and that other people are sleeping in doorways or drifting aimlessly, shuffling along in the shadows, sometimes clutching plastic carrier bags full of newspaper or sheets of cardboard, heads held down against wind or rain. It comes as a shock that first time; that moment when you discover that while the city sleeps there are still people, homeless, with nowhere to go.

This could be anywhere in Europe or the United States. Every major city has a similar problem. London or Paris, New York, Chicago or Leeds – they all have destitute people wandering their streets at night. The first time you see them you wonder why. How can it be, you ask yourself, with all the wealth at the world's command, that there are still human beings roofless and destitute, male and female, young and old, from every nation, with absolutely nowhere to call their own. They collect those bags of paper from waste bins or heaps of garbage left out by shopkeepers for early morning collection. Old newspapers stuffed between layers of old clothing provide

extra warmth against the cold night air. Cardboard
sheeting acts as a windshield. By morning it will all be
thrown away, stinking of urine and vomit, as the street
cleansers arrive to hose down the doorways and subways
where the homeless find shelter. For the cleansers it's a
filthy task for which they get extra pay.

Why are people reduced to this? They all had families,
didn't they? They all had mothers, homes and schools to
go to, didn't they? Wasn't the Welfare State set up to help
people like this? Our society provides places of shelter for
the abandoned child, for the mentally defective, for the
sick, the blind and the aged. So what goes wrong? Where
have these people come from?

The appalling truth is that no one knows how many
homeless people there are, although most authorities
agree that this is primarily a *city* problem and that
smaller communities somehow manage to find a place for
their misfits. Statistics for London have been gathered by
government departments, borough councils, voluntary
organisations and numerous researchers, but none of
them tallies and the people who work in this field have
different interpretations to thrust upon you. Some say
there are 30,000 homeless in London alone. Others put
the figure at 100,000. There are politicians looking for a
cause, volunteers searching for a career with a sense of
purpose, hucksters hustling for themselves (there's a lot
of money swilling around), and writers wrestling with a
social issue of untidy dimensions. Nothing is neat and
ordered. Everyone has their point to make. Frequently,
all too frequently, making the point becomes more important than the point itself. You have to leave your illusions
far behind if you try to help the homeless. They won't be
grateful. Why should they be? And what's your game
anyway? Playing with our consciences, are we? Trying to
ease the pain?

There are now people for whom Homelessness is a fine
career. Just like Race Relations or the Law. They can

study it at college or university and even write a Ph.D. Their local council may have a department of it, staffed by men and women whose salaries rise by one increment on the anniversary of their birth and whose offices are prettily festooned with decorations and fairy lights at Christmas. 'What's your boy going to do when he leaves university, Mrs Brown? Work for a housing charity? That's a good job, they tell me. Thirty-five hours a week, or less. Five weeks' holiday a year, or more – and if he ends up running one of those big London charities, he'll be on £25–30,000 a year, with a car and a pension. He should pay off his mortgage and be able to retire by the time he's 55 ... and it'll be such a nice job. He'll sit on Government committees and meet Prince Charles. It's nice for a young man to have a sense of vocation!'

And yet, despite the statistics, or lack of them; despite the career structures and vast sums of money now pumped into the homelessness industry by government departments and the Housing Corporation, and despite the genuine concern shown for the homeless by the Royal Family and the Church, they are still there, growing in number, walking the streets night and day, searching for a cup of coffee or a bowl of soup, provided by charities like St Mungo. They are the misfits of our modern world, people with nowhere to go, sometimes for the simple reason that they would rather not be bothered by all the worries that we find normal. For them this new homelessness industry is a strange joke. They have never heard of the Housing Corporation, capital allocations, revenue budgets or the bottom line. This money talk means nothing to them. Those Christmas lights in the Housing Department window are just one more indication that its doors are closed. All they want is a warm bed, something to eat, a cup of tea – and no questions asked.

That's what *we* find so hard to tolerate. We want to ask them questions. We want to know why they do it. We want to conduct our censuses to find out who they are and where they come from, and we want them to promise that they will move down to one of those comfy little flats that can be found so easily if they would only go to Barking, Dagenham or Andover via the kindly graces of the Government Mobility Scheme. Above all else, we want them to go away.

To tell the truth, we find them embarrassing, when we miss our last trains and come face to face with them, shuffling through the garbage or waiting in a patient queue at Charing Cross arches for a bowl of soup, looking so helplessly defiant; the living proof that something may be wrong with our modern world, and that perhaps we ought to change our values. We don't want to be told that 'the system' is breaking down or 'the problem' is getting worse, and that, now, well dressed beggars will accost you in Piccadilly or Regent Street in broad daylight, asking if you can spare fifty pence so that they can have a cup of tea or something to eat. Fifty pence! That's what they ask for these days. That's the true measure of inflation. Fifty pence. And every one has a different story to tell. Forget all those speeches about housing cuts, means tests and Jarrow marches. This is for real. We're down at the coal face now, here in the heart of one of the world's great cities, where young men and old, wearing suits, collars and ties, and short haircuts, will walk up to you and politely ask for fifty pence because they have nowhere to go, nowhere to live, no family to fall back on, and are looking ahead for an hour or so at a time, hoping to cadge enough money for egg and chips and a cup of tea, knowing that this can be spun out for half an hour in the warmth of a back street cafe.

They won't thank you for being told that there's a day centre in North Lambeth and another in Covent Garden. That's another world away, where questions are silently asked. All they want is food, warmth and a dry pair of shoes, because it's miserable walking the streets in the rain with feet wet and body soaking, and not a penny in the world.

It was like this in the days of Dickens and Orwell. Little changes from one generation to the next but the clothes we wear, the tools we use, the wars we wage and our measurements of social distress. And that's the sadness of it. All those good intentions down the drain. So much energy spent, and still so much to do.

Every few years the nation is shocked by new revelations of London's poverty. It was the novelist Charles Dickens who touched the early Victorian conscience with his all-too-truthful *Oliver Twist* (1837–8). The journalist Henry Mayhew, who founded *Punch*, brought us the first accurate descriptions of *London Labour and London Poor*, in four volumes published between 1851 and 1862. The social pioneers were led by William Booth who opened his first mission in Whitechapel, in 1865, and established the Salvation Army twelve years later. Since then politicians and clergymen of every hue have helped raise funds for the city's needy. Caring knows no religious boundary. Muslims, Catholics, Jews and Protestants can all be found working together among the London poor, but every now and then some new shock report jars the conscience, whether it be Charles Booth's *Life and Labour of the People in London* (1891–1903), George Orwell's *Down and Out in Paris and London* (1933) or *The Road to Wigan Pier* (1937), or, in more recent times, the Press revelations that came with the Rachman scandal (1963) and the Greve Report (1971), and the shocks delivered to the body politic by the force of such television programmes as *Cathy Come Home* (1967) or *Goodbye Longfellow Road* (1977).

Events like these often prompt committed pioneers to form a charity to remedy some recently identified social malaise, or to persuade Parliament that new legislation will provide a solution. Fashions change from year to year. Sometimes we are all asked to give generously to help those who are homeless through alcoholism. The next year, it may be drug addicts or the rent boys plying their trade in the West End amusement arcades. Battered wives were a great favourite, temporarily – and at the time of writing, victims of sexual abuse are guaranteed a charitable donation. This is a painful industry in which priorities compete, and in which those who work in one aspect really believe that their problem is more serious than the next.

All too often the original campaigning fervour dims until these fine new charities become a headache in themselves, turning into mini-bureaucracies, surrounded by their own red tape and the need to produce expensive publications and attractively printed annual reports, until their staff end up mouthing clichés for the Press, churning out doubtful statistics to keep prompting that vital flow of donations from elderly widows and kind-hearted old soldiers which pays their wages. In the saddest situations, and these are not uncommon in the charitable field, the staff spend most of their time fighting for higher wages and better working conditions. Management ends up justifying the existence of its organisation so as not to lose the grants from central and local government upon which all become dependent. And, eventually, the unpaid volunteers who serve on the executive committees and are legally responsible for the charities' finances and the proper conduct of their affairs find themselves deciding to hold a private meeting well away from the charity's offices to ask themselves the questions, 'Where are we going?', 'Why are we here?', 'Are we bankrupt?', 'What are we going to do about the staff?' or 'Shall we sack the director?'

One famous public figure agreed to become chairman of an equally well-known national charity in the early 1980s and held the post for two or three years until the day came when his temper snapped, and he walked into the head office, unannounced and unexpected, to find all the staff in yet another trade union meeting. He walked straight in and asked them all what they were doing. Having heard their reply, he said: 'Do you realise I have been coming down to this building, in my own time and at my own expense, for nearly three years because I was told of the work you did to help people who were homeless, and at every single meeting the main item on the agenda has been your pay and conditions. We never talk about the people we are supposed to be helping ...' He then walked out of the room, drove back to his office and wrote out his letter of resignation.

Not a word about that particular incident appeared in the Press, and that's often the way it goes. Most charities are able to function unhindered by the need to expose their affairs to public scrutiny. Occasionally, a crisis will hit the headlines – because a treasurer has vanished with the funds, or someone has had a sexual affair at the charity's expense – but such scandals are relatively rare. There are now 180,000 charities in Britain, and inevitably something goes wrong somewhere. Charities are no more perfect than any other man-made institution, but they straddle a strange no man's land between the activities of Manufacture, Commerce, Trade and State, exempt from many forms of taxation and barely accountable to the Charity Commission. Homelessness forms part of this much wider field. In addition, there are 2,600 housing associations registered with the Housing Corporation, receiving from the Corporation loans totalling £865,000,000 a year. (This figure is taken from the Housing Corporation's Annual Report for the year ending 31 March 1987.) These figures overlap to some extent because charities can also be registered as housing associations or as friendly societies, but overall the point is made: enormous sums of public money in the form of government grants passed on through the Housing Corporation from our taxes plus our own personal charitable donations are pouring into the Homelessness Industry.

And yet you can still miss a train at midnight, walk down a city street, and find fellow human beings sleeping in doorways, wrapped in cardboard and old newspaper, lying across hot air vents, or waiting outside the back door of some city restaurants to be given the food that you may have left at the side of your plate. (Some firms, like McDonald's, go even further and give away all unsold food at the end of the day.)

It's a depressing industry, Homelessness. So many people are trying so hard with so little to show for it. The good intentions are there. There is no shortage of kindness, but no one can measure the work that these charities do because they are dealing with clients who are often elusive, slipping from one agency to another, sometimes feckless, or maybe just plain afraid. Fear often drives a perfectly happy human being into homelessness. This seems unbelievable until you have studied their personal lives. We are all afraid of different terrors, yet it may be hard to comprehend the fear of one man who feels deeply frightened when he receives a court summons for pissing in the street. He may be afraid of his employers' reaction or what the neighbours will say when they read of his fine in the local paper; he may be afraid of going to court and the trappings of the legal system, and he may have a deep-down fear that he will lose his job or be laughed at by his friends or family. For this one man, his trivial offence may become an event of such startling proportions in his mind that he puts all the money he can find in his pocket and catches a train or hitches a lift to London, having heard (as people do) that you can vanish on its streets. Anyone who works for a central London housing charity can tell you of case histories similar to this, and of others much more serious – of men who have committed crimes of violence in a moment of temper, and then been terrified of what might happen to them; men who have left prison to find someone else has moved into their home and taken over their wives, children and worldly possessions; and others who have been just plain unlucky in this earthly battle for goods and chattels. Each one becomes an indefinable anonymous statistic, sometimes appearing on the files of many different charities, as he tries them all in a desperate search for food and shelter.

It is no good telling a man who has lost every single possession that he valued, and whose life has lost all meaning to him, that it was all his own fault. And it is no good trying to compare his values with yours; he may believe that the most important thing in the world to him, right now, is fifty pence for a cup of tea – and a second-hand pair of shoes, which may be starting to smell a bit, but which are a perfect joy to him because those hard rubber soles will keep his feet dry. At this moment his values are right for him, and if you are going to try to help him you had better believe it. Another thing that anyone working in a central London hostel will tell you is that their residents sleep fully dressed and wearing shoes because these are their most prized possessions, and may be stolen if left by their beds overnight. This is another world, my friend, that you begin to encounter when you miss that late night train and tread nervously through those very same streets that bear you daily. It's a world where men sometimes fight and may even kill each other over a pair of second-hand shoes, and if you want to help them you have to understand that they have values, too, and that some of them, not all, are desperately distressed by the circumstances in which they find themselves. They are not asking for your pity, but they would like fifty pence – and if you dare to go near them as they stand by that coffee stall they are just as likely to tell you to 'Bugger off!'

If we lived in a world that was governed by sense and logic, all that money channelled into public sector housing would provide enough homes for those who need them. But the world is not like that. It's a muddled place

where men miss their late night trains, wives lie at home
in bed and wonder where their husbands have got to,
destitute beings scrabble through dustbins, clergymen
sink to their knees searching for answers, and politicians
believe these can all be found in votes. In this strange,
wonderful, wholly irrational place, where so much
happens by chance, some men and women rise above it all
to provide a form of leadership that has nothing to do
with power or morality and everything to do with love.
They are just as bad as we are. They swear and drink and
sometimes lie, but they possess this quality that separ-
ates them from the rest of us. Sometimes they make as
big a mess of their lives as anyone else, but there is still
this part of them that is remarkable. It is no good trying
to make them cost-efficient because they work among the
homeless where there are always new pioneers on the
margins, tapping the available sources of funds, touching
the party political nerve.

This is like any other industry. It is competitive. People
win and people fail. Some get honours, knighthoods or
seats in Parliament. Some create institutions that take
their name, and thus achieve a form of immortality like
Mr Peabody. Others make an important contribution to
the problems of homelessness, and then get overtaken by
events. Some reach depths of disillusion as terrible as any
experienced by those pitiful men who throw away their
lives just because a policeman found them urinating in a
public place. This book describes a group of people whose
lives came together at certain times through the formation of one charity, the St Mungo Community Trust,
and the later development of another separate but
related organisation, the St Mungo Community Housing
Association. Some are now dead. Some have been
wounded. Some have been vilified. It is not a neat story
with a beginning and an end. They have never been
working in isolation. There have always been others
working elsewhere with similar hopes and anxieties.

For over a century the Salvation Army was the leading agency in this field. Nowadays eager young reformers tend to play down its role, but there are still over 100,000 British 'soldiers' carrying out between them an enormous programme of social work that embraces clubs for the over-60s, luncheon clubs, play groups, advice centres for young mothers and ex-prisoners, craft sessions, hostels for young girls, the elderly, or the homeless, in addition to their continuing work among the poor and destitute, which includes three London soup runs and others in provincial cities. Each night the Salvation Army provides beds for over 2,000 homeless people at its London hostels, and although these large Victorian buildings – such as those at Blackfriars and Great Peter Street, Westminster – may be far too large by modern criteria, they nevertheless provide a facility that is desperately needed. In addition, the Salvation Army sustains a programme of ancillary work – essential in helping the homeless resettle within the community – through its rehabilitation units for alcoholics (there are two in London and others in Scotland, Wiltshire, Yorkshire, Nottingham and Southampton). The Army also provides a nationwide advice service for people leaving prison.

Similar programmes of work are also organised within the Church of England and by Roman Catholics, although not on such a diverse nationwide scale. Church Army Housing maintains five large hostels for men in London and also one for women, while Catholic effort is largely channelled through individual charities like the Providence Row refuge (which has been established for over a hundred years), or the Societies of St Vincent and of St Martin of Tours, which maintain individual hostels that are often much smaller than those run by the Salvation Army, and somewhat less regimented – their success often depends largely upon the character of the individual warden. There is one London hostel (which I am not going to identify because this might damage the work done there) that regularly accepts homeless people after they have been turned away *everywhere* else for reasons that even the most sympathetic social worker would understand; its residents include those who have served long prison sentences for murder, rape and other acts of personal violence. This hostel has been established through the work of a former Catholic priest who happened to fall in love with a woman, abandoned his vows of celibacy, gave up the priesthood, married her and now has a large family of children. His days have been spent working within this small community of men whose crimes have left them without home or family. It is an extraordinarily happy place. Some of its residents do end up back in prison but others resettle back into the community, finding new family relationships and making a fresh start in life.

There is also another community where men who have committed horrible sexual offences against women and children are helped to find a new place in society. We are all so appalled by these crimes when we read of them in the Press that we tend to forget that the judicial process is such that one morning the gaol doors will open at 8 am and these men will be turned out into the street, their sentences completed. I knew of one case where a man was released from prison in his mid-60s, having spent nearly fifty years of his life in gaol for violating other people's children. Every time he had been released from prison he had always done it again, and now here he was, at the age of 66, finishing his latest term and being turned out on to the streets again. The likelihood was that some poor child would be abused within a matter of days, but according to the law his sentence was up and out he went.

Make no mistake; that man was homeless. Can you imagine any family welcoming him back? Nobody wanted him, but somebody had to help him – and the staff running this second project do just that, counselling sex offenders, helping them find work and accommodation, and, if their problem is a medical one, advising them on the drugs that are now available to reduce libido. (This is one of the untold success stories of recent times. There are now men living within the community, some happily married, who have been able to curb their violent sexual impulses through the use of drugs that restore the imbalance in their hormones.) There are several projects like this in Britain, necessarily maintaining a low profile. Often their clients have had other problems as well, such as alcoholism, drug addiction, mental retardation, mental illness or some physical deformity, and their need is desperate. What they have done has damaged whatever family life they may have had, and the first essential is to provide a caring environment within which they can restructure their lives.

It would be a mistake to assume that all the people you see sleeping in doorways or begging for money on the city streets have problems as severe as these, but some do – and almost all of them need careful counselling to ascertain why they are homeless, and what has gone wrong with their lives. This highly skilled work is an essential part of the rehousing process. Those who have lost their homes and family, whether they be men or women, may have lost not just the will to live but the desire to maintain those personal everyday values which most of us take for granted. Once people fall to this level of desperation their lives may deteriorate very quickly. Because they have no address they cannot get money from the DHSS. And because they have no money they cannot rent a bed. A major part of each day is spent walking the streets. To avoid having to carry possessions they either sell or throw away whatever they may have left, and soon they are reduced to just the clothing they wear. Keeping clean becomes a problem. Before very long their hair is growing longer, their skin is becoming dirtier, and they are starting to smell. They know this is happening to them, but there is nothing much they can do about it

because the poorer they get the harder it is to survive –
and it's a very short journey to Skid Row. By then their
hair is hanging, thick, dank and matted; their boots have
rotted; their clothes and bodies have a smell that's as
unmistakable as gangrene, and the odds are that unless
someone rescues them *quickly* they'll be found one
morning lying in a doorway, an unpleasant heap of skin
and bone, covered in flies and lice.

Those words were not written lightly; you have to leave
your illusions behind if you want to help people like this,
and that is what men like that former priest have done in
committing their lives to this work. And it's not just
Catholics or Salvation Army 'soldiers' or the men and
women of the Church Army. There are Jewish hostels in
London, too, and some of the finest missions in the East
End have been built up over the past sixty or seventy
years by Methodists and other Nonconformists. And
there have been individual pioneers, too, like Anton
Wallich-Clifford and Richard Carr-Gomm who have
brought a purely personal insight to this work. It was
Wallich-Clifford who established the first Simon Community in 1963, and these communities – like those also run
by the Cyrenians in over fifty towns and cities – provide a
settled but austere life for the formerly homeless, with
staff and residents subsisting on similar incomes, jointly
running each community together. Richard Carr-Gomm
had a slightly different vision, establishing another
nationwide chain of 'houses' run by fifteen separate local
groups within one overall Society, providing between
them over 500 bedrooms. For Richard Carr-Gomm, the
initial purpose was to help the lonely; for others, it has
been the more specialised aims mentioned earlier, but
they all form part of a wider whole. Homelessness is such
a complex problem that they all have a part to play, and
yet . . . you can still walk the streets at midnight and find
people with nowhere to go.

Chapter 2

All social movements have some moment in their history when their course changed. For the homeless the sixties were a crucial period when society seemed to become more aware of their plight. Volunteers from many different professions and occupations began making a contribution, either by raising funds, spending an evening or two a week helping to man an advice agency, or by working in a hostel.

Until then the post-war years had been accompanied by a building boom. As Churchill's Housing Minister, Harold Macmillan had gained the reputation for getting things done and this had propelled him into Downing Street. Macmillan had overseen a programme that provided over 300,000 new homes a year. By the early sixties there was a nice comfortable feeling abroad that Britain was a well-housed prosperous nation that was doing rather well for itself, with food a-plenty and television sets and washing machines in nearly every home. The clichés of the age, 'You've never had it so good' and 'I'm all right, Jack', summarised the prevailing attitude well. There was a feeling of self-satisfaction in the air as Britain disentangled itself from its obligations in Africa, Asia and the Middle East, gradually lowering its expectations until, as Dean Acheson put it, the nation found itself with neither an empire nor a role. The bubble was shattered in 1963 by what was loosely called the Profumo scandal.

Like all the most enduring scandals, this one unfolded slowly with rumours spreading around the Westminster bars about different politicians who were believed to be sleeping with tarts or walking around half-naked at smart society parties. Many were the names that were mentioned, and, briefly, a sad parade of minor celebrities

had their lives torn apart by the courts and Press, while
the moralists had a wonderful time telling us all how bad
it was. The scandal itself did not amount to much. A
rising young Conservative Minister, married to a beautiful actress, made love to a pretty young girl who had also
slept with one or two other people (including the Russian
Naval Attaché). She had a friend who also enjoyed going
to parties. That was all it really boiled down to, but there
were the usual bit-part players in this tacky drama – the
pimps who wanted a slice of the action, the tarts with a
story to sell, and the politicians-on-the-make who saw
this 'security scandal' as an opportunity to take pot-shots
at a Prime Minister who was nearing the end of his term
of office. However, what began as a sex scandal slowly
turned into something much more exciting; a real crisis of
confidence – because it became clear to the electorate that
the Prime Minister did not know how to handle his Ministers, and the situation itself revealed that there were
some rather unsavoury people on the fringes of London
Society who made their living exploiting the homeless.
The key figure was Peter Rachman who had lived with
that other girl who liked going to parties.

In normal times this scandal might have fizzled away,
like they mostly do, but these were not. Four years had
passed since the last General Election. The date was
approaching when the Government had to face the
electorate.

Ben Parkin, a much respected Labour MP, pecked
away at the Rachman aspect of the affair. He had every
right to do so. Rachman was buying up property in
Parkin's constituency and making people homeless.
Against that background of a large building programme,
the Government had felt able to pass the 1957 Rent Act
believing that this would 'free up' the housing market. It
was argued that there were sufficient homes available for
the State to begin removing the rights of tenure that
occupants of privately rented housing had possessed since

the middle of the First World War. These rights had been given originally to ease domestic stress during wartime, but by 1957 it had become apparent that many private tenants were paying so little rent that their landlords did not receive enough income to maintain their properties. Houses were falling into disrepair, and tenants were reluctant to move because they would lose their security of tenure and have to pay a higher rent. In theory, the Act sounds sensible enough – but in areas like Paddington (which Parkin represented) these privately rented houses were vast early Victorian buildings, with as many as twenty or thirty rooms. Rachman realised he could buy them cheaply because they had sitting tenants – and then all he had to do was get the tenants out and let the properties off room by room. Each house could become a little goldmine. The problem was getting the tenants out but Rachman solved that by bringing in thugs with alsatians and crowbars. Similarly, he made sure that his new tenants – who were often black or poor – paid high rents and did not complain. Parkin raised all this in Parliament, and then the Press moved in, exposing Rachman as a racketeer. His name and the manner in which he built up his housing empire brought a new word to the English language – Rachmanism.

The exposure of Rachman coincided with the Profumo scandal, and because he had known some of the characters in that drama (and had lived with one of the girls) the two scandals merged into one crisis of confidence in the Macmillan Government. The electorate was genuinely shocked, not so much by the sexual revelations as the impression created of a society drifting into dissolute chaos with the Prime Minister helpless, Ministers whoring and peers and politicians swirling in decadence while crooks and speculators exploited the poor.

With a General Election only months away, and the Government's rating plummeting in the opinion polls, the political atmosphere became highly charged. Tempo-

rarily, homelessness became a major issue. Shock photo-
graphs appeared in the Press and on television of women
and children who were undernourished and had nowhere
decent to live. Similar artwork was employed for political
posters. Angry debates were held in the House of
Commons. Speeches rattled around the town hall council
chambers. The post-war dream was over.

In situations like these, attitudes vary. Some reach for
the sick bag. Others join a political party to work for
change. Some, just a few, move out of the mainstream to
become personally involved. That was what happened in
the early sixties in the wake of the Rachman scandal. It
was then that Anton Wallich-Clifford established his first
Simon Community, and the Revd Austen Williams, then
Vicar of St Martin in the Fields, founded the National
Association of Voluntary Hostels which linked many voluntary agencies through one central referral point. At
their offices in Covent Garden, NAVH kept a register of
all the available bedspaces to help other charities who
were trying to find accommodation for homeless people
with particular personal problems.

In founding the Simon Community, Anton Wallich-
Clifford was driven by the profoundly Christian ideal
that Homelessness must be met on the streets as a
problem with a personal face. The idea had the smack of
John Bunyan's *Pilgrim's Progress* about it. The underlying belief was that homeless people should be
encountered on their own territory through providing a
soup run and then be invited to give up their rootless
existence to share basic living accommodation with the
community 'workers'. Each community would share a
small run-down house with the workers receiving a
minimal wage and they would all live together, sharing
the cooking and cleaning, and all the decisions that
governed their lives. Many thousands of people have
lived in such homes since then and there are many who
believe that this is the most effective way of helping the

homeless. The other side of the coin is that the standards maintained are often low with workers taking something akin to a vow of poverty, receiving just a little pocket money and wearing second-hand clothes. The rejection of material values began as a fine ideal but all too often degenerated into a form of proselytising that was both religious and politically evangelical. Disputes became a characteristic of the Simon communities, and one of these schisms gave birth to St Mungo in 1969.

Throughout the sixties homelessness was growing in London, and so were people's perception of the problem. In 1967, the nation was moved to tears by Jeremy Sandford's BBC TV play *Cathy Come Home* which showed a young couple losing their home and their children after a series of everyday crises with which millions of viewers could identify. This programme was shown twice on television and brought into everyone's home the reality of homelessness; the bailiffs called in to enforce evictions; the squalor in many council-run hostels for homeless families, and the dereliction in which some families were forced to live. The public response was generous. Over £1m a year was donated to the charity Shelter which channelled the money into various projects providing short-term accommodation and itself became a vigorous (and sometimes raucous) campaigning organisation.

Briefly, homelessness was at the forefront of political debate. The London Boroughs Association and the Greater London Council, which rarely worked together in a spirit of harmony, studied the problem at great length, setting up a working party which recommended that the responsibility for homelessness should be transferred from social services departments to housing. (This was gradually implemented by the boroughs, and eventually became national policy with the 1974 reorganisation of local government.) The mood was changing. With the establishment of new larger local authorities and the Housing Corporation being given greater powers to fund and encourage the growth of the voluntary movement, the politicians thought their work was done. Housing slipped back down the political agenda.

Of course, nothing had really changed. It rarely does. Parliament may shuffle functions from this department to that. New local authorities may be set up to streamline administration. But, at the end of the day, homelessness is about people who reject all these neat political formulae ... and the sad truth was that homelessness grew steadily worse during the very period when the politicians were convincing themselves that the problem was easing. All these fine new charities found themselves lurching from crisis to crisis faced with the recurrent problem of raising funds to pay their own wage bills, and within those agencies where there was a strong sense of moral purpose there was all too frequently an equally strong sense of political fervour. Smart young activists with university degrees sat poised by their telephones beneath strike posters and busts of Lenin, and if you tried to dial their number it was either engaged, off the hook or connected to an answering machine. Those were the years when the new young councillors started voting grants through to help these charities on their way. We were all sincere; this was the way we would solve the problem. But we didn't!

On one night in October 1972, the St Mungo Community Trust carried out a survey of the streets of London and found 12,000 single homeless people with nowhere to go. That same year another charity, New Horizon, estimated that there were 8,000 young people sleeping rough in London, and that 20 per cent were girls. The problem was getting worse. All the signs were there ... in 1971, a Rowton House hostel for men was closed in the Elephant and Castle district of Lambeth to make way for yet another high rise development of flats and offices, and another 880 beds were lost. Later Rowton closed their hostel at Butterwick in Hammersmith with the loss of a further 750 beds. These were never replaced. London's population was declining, and its politicians were told there were beds to spare at the Salvation Army. In truth, the problem was getting inexorably worse as patterns of occupation changed in both public and private sectors.[1] This was exacerbated as the early seventies property boom gathered momentum with developers clearing many inner areas of early Victorian housing which had been providing the city's cheapest hotel, hostel and lodging house accommodation. It all seemed so progressive at the time; old buildings swept away so that tall blocks of flats could be erected in their place. Better homes for everyone, the Ministers said.

There were always some siren voices saying that government and local government priorities were going wrong. One of them belonged to a man named Jim Horne, who had been a Simon Community worker during the sixties and was now running the St Mungo Community Trust. Jim Horne was a rough diamond. Like many Simon Community workers he had been in trouble with the law. His background was always a mystery, but over the years that followed it was learned that he had at different times experienced what was euphemistically called 'Borstal training', that he had left the Army under a cloud, had been a patient at the Henderson psychiatric hospital in South London, and had also read psychology at Glasgow University. According to a later article by Harold Atkins in *The Daily Telegraph* (31 October 1977):

Mr Horne had an extraordinary introduction to his spirited incursion into London social work. 'I was four years out of the

---

[1] This is one of the factors that complicate any discussion of homelessness. The GLC Research Department analysed the Census statistics for 1961 and 1971 and found that the net annual decline in London's population was over 100,000 a year while the actual housing stock was slowly increasing. However, this coincided with a trend towards smaller families and an increase in the numbers of single people living alone in self-contained accommodation, and the shift in population did not ease the problems of the homeless.

Army,' he told me, 'with a drug and drink problem that got me into dossing in London myself.

'One night eleven years ago I fell down a flight of steps into the basement of a derelict house and broke both legs.

'I found myself in a sort of *Macbeth* witches' kitchen, as I thought, with three weird figures and a fire going. They were meths drinkers – all men – and they were kind to the new arrival. They gave me food and looked after me down there for five weeks.

'I wouldn't go to hospital but when at last I was taken to St Thomas's they visited me. It was the first time I'd experienced real friendship in my life and it moved me very much.'

When a year or so later, with his drink-drugs problem over, he returned to London after reading some psychology at Glasgow University, he found that two of them were dead, the third dying of cancer. This one talked about his friends – mostly Scots drinking groups out of the Services. 'I was appalled at a lot of it. I decided to do something.'

Initially, in 1968, Jim Horne became a worker with the Simon Community, wearing old clothes like the rest of them and his hair long and bedraggled, as he pushed an old pram holding a large container of soup around the London streets.

One day he was stopped by a suspicious policeman who thought he was drug-running. On the spur of the moment, he muttered something about St Mungo and the policeman immediately responded by calling him 'Sir', obviously assuming that anyone who could mention the name of a saint must be a clergyman either down on his luck or doing something useful.[2]

Horne was a man of great energy with natural skills as a publicist, and before long became the right-hand man to

---

[2] Among Glaswegians, 'Mungo' is a term of endearment like 'Cobber' to an Australian or 'Mate' to an East Ender. It was the nickname for St Kentigern, a little-known saint who was born in Lothian, then part of Northumbria, in the middle of the sixth century AD. He was a great missionary in the North of England and then later in Wales where he

Jim Horne

Anton Wallich-Clifford. When that schism came in 1969, Horne emerged from the embroglio in possession of the house in which he was living and a van that had been acquired to supply more soup to the city's vagrants than he had been able to carry in his pram. Every morning he would drive down to Smithfield Market to pick up van loads of free bones with which to make soup stock. He would also pick up large quantities of unwanted vegetables at Covent Garden, and in semi-derelict buildings acquired from the GLC and other local authorities for just token rents he set up his own soup kitchens. Soon he had volunteers working with him for just pocket money, and began acquiring a group of run-down houses (always for just a token rent from local authorities) which he used for accommodating the dossers who were met on the soup run. Conditions were rough with shabby second-hand furnishings and bedding, but this was shelter for destitute men and women; somewhere they could bed down for the night, or longer, without too many questions being asked, and an address to enable them to qualify for subsistence payments from the Department of Health and Social Security.

From those small beginnings came the St Mungo Community Trust and the St Mungo Community Housing Association. Over the next ten years Horne was to become the most charismatic figure working among the London homeless, gathering around him a team of devoted (though often volatile) volunteers, and using all those publicity skills to wheedle large sums of public money from government departments and local authorities. His persistence was legendary. Before obtaining St Mungo's first grant from the Department of Health and

established a monastery at Llanelwy. He is said to have performed many miracles including the rescue of an unfaithful queen from the anger of her husband, and is most closely associated with Glasgow where he is said to have been the first bishop. The city's heraldic arms bear a ring and a fish in memory of him, and his reputed tomb is in Glasgow Cathedral.

Social Security he managed to persuade the Permanent Under Secretary, Mary Jones, to go out on his soup run – and then the Secretary of State, Sir Keith Joseph, went too. St Mungo also held a party every year at Battersea Town Hall to which he invited hundreds of guests, including civil servants, local councillors amd Members of Parliament. When Barbara Castle became the new Secretary of State after the General Election in February 1974, one of the first sights to greet her as she moved into her suite at the DHSS offices at the Elephant and Castle was a bouquet of flowers from Jim Horne. By then he had become the right man in the right place at the right time to do something new to help the London homeless.

Less than twelve months earlier, power had changed hands at County Hall. In what were then the triennial Greater London Council elections, the Conservatives had been defeated after holding office for six years and the new Labour administration had been working closely with their parliamentary colleagues in readiness for the General Election. He may not have known it, but all the cards were falling right for Jim Horne. That new GLC administration included one man, Paddy O'Connor, who really did want to help the London poor, and another, Illtyd Harrington, a fellow Roman Catholic, who controlled the Council's purse strings and was prepared to support O'Connor within the Labour Group. The GLC had been established less than ten years earlier with no welfare powers; there never had been any attempt by local government to house the poorest of the single homeless, and now both the London Boroughs Association and the Government were accepting that this was a function best exercised by housing departments. By an accident of parliamentary fate the GLC had been designated a *strategic* housing authority with London-wide responsibility – and these unique powers had never been properly defined.

Chapter 3

Paddy O'Connor was no saint. There was nothing mystical or evangelical about this man. He was a tough, bloody-minded, hard-drinking Irishman who felt at home in that rough Catholic working-class underworld that forms such an important part of the London Labour movement.

In recent years, the Press has claimed that the London Labour Party is in the grip of Militants and other young extremists. It has never been as simple as that. No one man or faction can control a movement that is as broadly based as this with trade union branches in many crafts, strong sections in the construction industry and London Regional Transport, a wide range of women's organisations (including some that are lesbian-led but many more that are dominated by old ladies who like making tea on election days), and a wide-ranging general membership. It is one of the Labour Party's rules that people must join the local branch that geographically covers the area in which they live, and in London's concentrated residential districts this means that there are some local parties that are packed with Members of Parliament, civil servants, City executives, young professionals, college lecturers or students, and almost every nationality under the sun – it has been estimated that there are now 170 languages spoken in Greater London! Within this movement many different philosophies parade beneath the broad banner of Socialism, and the most that any one group can hope for is that they may, temporarily, hold sway while a candidate is chosen for a local council election or the parliamentary seat.

This fragmentation is a relatively recent phenomenon. For most of this century the Catholics have been one of Labour's most powerful forces, particularly in the old

East End boroughs and among the tightly knit estates that lie just to the north of London's commercial core. Walk through these areas and you will find statuettes of the Virgin Mary and the infant Jesus on nearly every living-room wall. Within this community, which comes together through a network of pubs, clubs and churches, the southern Irish have long been dominant. They provide its priests and much of its lifeblood, being mostly employed on the city's building sites, in the large central hospitals, on the Underground and in the regional bus depots. Paddy O'Connor knew this area well; it was his political base, and its different threads ran parallel with those of his own life.

By the time I knew him, Paddy O'Connor was in his 50s. He was every bit as rough a diamond as Jim Horne, although he had that special Irish lilt and a gift for comradeship. He could be unreliable. I am sure of that. After he died some of his colleagues talked sadly of his darker deeds and the times they had 'covered' for him when Paddy had stepped with too much daring along the boundaries of the law.

Luke Patrick O'Connor was born on 22 August 1916 in the small town of Bray in County Wicklow, seven miles outside Dublin. His parents, Mick and Katie, had five children of whom Paddy was the second. He left school when he was 14 years old, and two years later, in the summer of 1932, travelled to London with 7s 6d (41p) in his pocket. To begin with he washed dishes, scrubbed floors and slept rough on the Embankment, although in later years he would admit that this had been no great hardship because the weather was warm and dry. Nevertheless, it was an experience that he never forgot – just as he never forgot his spell in prison. I can't remember now why he ended up in gaol, although he did tell me once, but what I do recall is the tone of his reminiscences. As a southern Irishman, Paddy was a natural Republican, and identified with the cause of the IRA without necessarily

Paddy O'Connor

approving of violence. He was in a prison cell the night before one of their men was hanged. It was a memory that lived with him for the rest of his days, and one afternoon, when he had drunk far too much whisky, it all came pouring out in a cascading flow of emotion and rhetoric. There was no bitterness, just a feeling of pain, as he recalled the angry clatter of chamber pots and baccy cans on the prison bars that suddenly stopped the moment they all knew that one of their number was walking through to the execution shed, and then the minutes of terrifying silence.

Like many Irishmen, Paddy fought for Britain during the Second World War, serving with the RAF as a rear gunner, based in North Africa. He then worked in a Luton car factory before becoming a London Transport bus conductor, a driver and finally a staff instructor. His politics were pure and simple. For some years he was a Communist and then switched to Labour, becoming Chairman of the St Pancras Housing Committee before the borough was swallowed up by Camden in the local government reorganisation of 1963–5. He was a rumbustious councillor, and for many years was surcharged ten shillings a week from his wages as a result of the St Pancras refusal to increase rents (which brought them into conflict with the District Auditor). Later, as Mayor of Camden, he visited the Soviet Union as a guest of the Russian leader, Aleksei Kosygin, and once was arrested by the police for causing an obstruction. He was campaigning for a pedestrian crossing in Robert Street for the safety of children. His arrest caused a great sensation in the London Press; that wasn't the way Mayors were supposed to behave – but Paddy got his crossing!

It was a broadcast on London radio, in 1973, that brought him into the homeless field. Jim Horne was interviewed for the same programme, and challenged Paddy to join him out on the nightly soup run to see the conditions endured by the city's homeless for himself.

Illtyd Harrington went with them on a bitterly cold October night. News of their visit quickly spread, and the following day they were both pressed for comments.[1] 'London has a harrowing problem on its hands,' said Harrington. 'I have seen nothing quite as pitiful since I was in Algiers with the RAF,' said Paddy. Between them they had the power to do something about it. Harrington was Deputy Leader of the Council and controlled its budget; O'Connor was Deputy Chief Whip. When they called for action, the Council's officers responded – and within a month the GLC had found the old Marmite factory in Durham Street, Kennington, which was made available to the St Mungo Trust.

The Council Leader, the late Sir Reg Goodwin, and the Labour Group then gave Paddy the power to carry out what became a one-man programme of social reform. It was an astonishing exercise. He was allowed a budget of £50,000 a year, which was more or less under his personal control, and permitted the use of a Council car and chauffeur. Some weeks later, a Single Homeless Subcommittee of the Housing Development Committee was set up to give this arrangement some authority. Briefly, it had four members. Paddy, an elderly member named Fred Archer, Ken Livingstone – and me. They were the Labour Party and took the decisions; I was the Conservative Party – and led the Opposition!

Seldom in the history of local government can there have been an oddball enterprise quite like it. The Standing Orders of the GLC were such that once policy decisions had been taken, responsibility for their execution lay with the individual Committee chairmen, who would work closely with the Council officers concerned and were themselves answerable to the Council. A tough chairman, or a wily one, could influence the course of events

---

[1] At that time there were two London evening newspapers, the *Evening News* and the *Evening Standard*, which both had reporters permanently based at County Hall, where the BBC and LBC also had their own radio studios. An event like this therefore received instant news coverage.

decisively – and work away at his own pace without much fear of any outside intervention. Provided they believed that the chairman had the support of his colleagues, the officers would accept his instructions. Paddy drove through this loophole with a coach and horses, spending money without proper authority from the very first day.

Because my sympathies lay wholly with what he was trying to do, the Labour Party went out of its way to keep me properly informed even when Paddy was causing them great embarrassment. Outside the Council Chamber, Goodwin, Harrington or the Labour Chief Whip, Harvey Hinds, would take me on one side, tell me of his latest misadventure, either grinning or rolling their eyes as they prefaced each story with a phrase like, 'Paddy's gone off the rails again . . . we're having a hell of a time with him.'

Superficially, this may sound as if they were trying to compromise me (which they may have been), but it was more complex than that. Lloyd George once said that if you wanted to get a dirty job done you had to get a dirty pair of hands, and none of us was in any doubt that dealing with the dossers on the London Embankment came within this category, but Paddy was so determined to help them that he flouted every normal restraint or convention.

This soft-hearted, drunken Irishman would go careering off down to the East End of London in his Council car, looking for empty houses, setting up 'hostels', picking up dossers and down-and-outs, and then dropping them into St Mungo's night shelters. This wasn't his own private car. Other officials were allowed to use it as well, and there were frequent complaints about the smell. Some nights he would be out on the soup run, handling the ladle – and when he had finished his night's work his chauffeur would drop him at some all-night Catholic drinking club where Paddy would join his friends at the bar, and there he would stand, always with a fag in the corner of his mouth, telling stories and drinking whisky until it closed. For all this he was claiming the expenses he was entitled to for hours spent on Council business. It broke all the accepted rules of local government. There were no committee decisions; no authorisation for all these little odd items of expenditure. We all did what we could to control him. Paddy was told that every single car trip would have to be sanctioned in advance, and all expenditure properly certified, but now we were dealing with a man with a mission who was determined to break through all the red tape that surrounded the Council's work. Anyone who stood in his way, be they Labour or Conservative, was 'just another fucking Tory' who didn't understand the problems he was trying to solve. And, let's face it, the vast majority of those whom he was trying to help were working-class people who had at one point in their lives fallen on hard times, and didn't know how to work the system in the way that a middle-class person would, without thinking.

For nearly three years it has to be admitted that the Council may have broken the law. There was no proper legal authorisation for this work. When passing the 1963 London Government Act, Parliament did not give the GLC powers to deal with single homelessness. As explained already, the boroughs were busily shuffling responsibility for homelessness between their social services and housing departments, some willingly and some reluctantly – but this was only for *families*.

Once Paddy O'Connor began charging through the local governmment dovecotes it was discovered that there was some doubt as to whether or not *any* local authority had any legal powers to help the *single* homeless. The lawyers began combing through the Housing and Social Services legislation of the past thirty years and uncovered a fine old muddle. Of course, nobody told the Press (no one ever does), but it transpired that we were all breaking the law in trying to provide some comfort for those poor men and women who could be found shuffling through London's garbage and sleeping in its doorways.

As usually happens in situations like these, where party politicians agree that their backs need protecting, discussions took place between the lawyers of the GLC, the London Boroughs and the Department of the Environment, and the Department of Health and Social Security. A careful study of the pages of Hansard will reveal the following statement by the then Secretary of State for the Environment, Anthony Crosland, on 10 June 1974:

Mr Douglas-Mann asked the Secretary of State for the Environment whether he is now in a position to make a statement about the statutory responsibility of local authorities to provide temporary accommodation for the homeless.

Mr Crosland: Yes, local authorities have a statutory duty under Section 21(1)(b) of the National Assistance Act 1948 to provide temporary accommodation for those in urgent need of it, in the circumstances set out in that Act.

I recognise – indeed, once shared – the concern which has been expressed, notably by Members of this House and by a number of voluntary bodies, about the effect on that duty of changes made by the Local Government Act 1972. I want, therefore, to put it on record clearly that that duty remains in full force. It lies, as it has done since 1948, in the social services authority. Under the 1948 Act the duty to provide temporary accommodation for the homeless was mandatory. Under the Local Government Act 1972 it became a permissive power, but subject to powers of direction by the Secretary of State for Social Services, which could make it mandatory. Such a direction was issued on 11th February 1974.

The fact that the duty now rests on a direction does not diminish its effect in law; the direction itself was issued under statute. My Right Hon. Friend the Secretary of State for Social Services has asked me to say that she does not intend to withdraw that direction, made by her predecessor in the previous administration, and neither of us can conceive that any Secretary of State would withdraw it,

I make this statement with the intention of putting to rest any doubts or misgivings on this technical aspect of an important social duty. However, neither my Right Hon. Friend the Secretary of State for Social Services nor I am satisfied that this Government should rest simply on the basis of existing legislation in respect of the duties and powers of either social services or housing authorities. We intend, on the basis of the consideration we have given to the issues which arise on homelessness and of the representations put to us, to initiate a wide-ranging review in consultation with the local authority associations and representative voluntary organisations. This will cover the need for new legislation relating to the functions of housing and social services authorities in relation to homelessness; the spread of the financial, administrative and management responsibilities of these authorities; and any other related matters which are put forward by the Government, the local authority associations or the voluntary bodies.

We are determined to avoid a legalistic approach to what are essentially human problems. Statutory duties and powers will not, of themselves, enable local authorities to do more for the homeless, whether by way of providing more temporary accommodation or more houses, or of making other services available. We appreciate the need for a clearly understood framework of responsibilities backed by law, and this will be a main object of the review. But we must take account of the regional and national character of the homelessness problem; of the fact that the housing situation which we inherited was appalling and cannot, despite the range of measures I have already announced, be improved overnight; and of the situation of those authorities in whose areas homelessness is an increasing problem but who are faced also with the whole complex of other housing needs which only they can take and lead in tackling

Meanwhile, my Right Hon. Friend the Secretary of State for Social Services and I wish to make it unequivocally clear that we expect local authorities to make the best use of their combined housing and social services resources; to exercise all their existing duties and powers; and to deal effectively and compassionately with the needs of those who are or are in danger of becoming homeless, in accordance with our Departments' circulars of February 1974.

This careful statement, expressed in the usual parliamentary jargon, was intended to protect us all from the risk of prosecution or surcharge by the District Auditor, should a ratepayer draw his attention to the fact that the GLC was spending public money without proper legal authority. That 'wide-ranging review' never happened – but three years later this situation was formally resolved when the Government agreed to propose an amendment to the Homeless Persons Bill, which was then being steered through the House of Commons as a private members' measure by the Liberal MP Stephen Ross. This amendment, which became Section 13 of the Housing (Homeless Persons) Act 1977, finally gave legal sanction for any local authority that wanted to use its housing powers to give grants to voluntary organisations like St Mungo that were seeking to help the homeless.

Meanwhile, the irrepressible Paddy O'Connor had steered funds and buildings in the direction of St Mungo and other new charities which were also prepared to bust a muscle or maybe break a law to provide beds and food for London's dossers. Some major national companies showed great kindness. Heinz donated the soup that was given away each night by the St Mungo workers. Mazda donated a van. Businessmen and lawyers offered free advice. The GLC allocated staff to the programme and ensured that semi-derelict houses were made available to provide short-term accommodation, before being used eventually for road widening purposes or the development of new housing estates.

All this had begun with that exercise down at the Marmite factory in the late autumn of 1973. Paddy O'Connor had heard that this large derelict building was standing empty. Down he went in that Council car, and then he contacted the owners who agreed that the premises could be made available through the GLC for emergency accommodation for the homeless over that Christmas. St Mungo was brought in to provide a volunteer staff. Hotels and hospitals were asked to provide any unwanted beds or second-hand mattresses. Manufacturers were asked to provide free food, and nobody stopped to think about such trifles as planning consent, fire precautions, the legislation covering safety at work, the Health Acts, or the fact that the sewers had never been intended to carry the waste of several hundred people.[2] Conditions were chaotic, but that Christmas over a thousand people were provided with food and shelter.

As a one-man initiative, this was a small incident in the history of London's affairs; it happened during a winter when the miners and power workers were out on strike, and millions of homes were plunged into darkness by electricity cuts. Homelessness generally was increasing; figures released by the DHSS[3] showed that the numbers of London *families* accommodated in bed-and-breakfast hotels and boarding houses had more than doubled, and that at the latest date there were 767 homeless families sheltered in this way, representing some 2,402 people. These were families with children, for whom the councils had a legal responsibility under Section 21 (1)(b) of the National Assistance Act 1948. The figures did not include the many thousands of *single* homeless people for whom no one would accept responsibility. For them the temporary shelter provided at the

---

[2] It was reported on *The London Programme* (LWT) that Horne dealt with the sewer problem in characteristic fashion. One Sunday morning, traffic signs appeared saying the road was closed; a gang of men appeared to dig up the road; new pipes were laid; the road surface was restored – and away they went. No one bothered to tell the local council.

[3] These figures are taken from Press Release No. 31 issued by the London Boroughs Association on 29 November 1973, quoting DHSS statistics and the boroughs' response. The statistics were for the six-month period ending June 1973.

Marmite factory and the parallel work being done in what were still its early days by the charity Crisis at Christmas were a godsend. And as the New Year began, Paddy O'Connor put down his foot and said the Marmite factory would not close. He had no authority for saying it, but on 3 January 1974 the following Press statement was issued by the GLC Press Office on his instructions:

FACTORY SHELTER FOR THE DOWN-AND-OUTS WILL NOT CLOSE, SAY GLC, UNTIL ALTERNATIVE ACCOMMODATION FOUND

Shelter provided by the Greater London Council for the down-and-outs housed over a thousand single homeless during Christmas, and every night since nearly 300 bed down in the disused factory at 1–31 (odd) Durham Street, Kennington.

Mr Paddy O'Connor, GLC Alderman, who has special responsibilities for GLC policy on London's down-and-outs said today: 'I am very pleased that the factory has been such a success. It's not of course ideal, but it fills a very desperate need, and we have no intention of closing it and putting these people on the streets until we have alternative shelter for them.

'I have appealed to Sir Keith Joseph, Minister of the Department of Health and Social Security, to release the disused wing of the Charing Cross Hospital. It is in an excellent position in central London where many down-and-outs congregate.

'We need to give these single homeless all the help we can. We must keep them off the streets permanently.'

The down-and-outs are being looked after by the St Mungo Trust Charity, and during Christmas the Trust threw a three-day party at the factory, with turkey, plum pudding and other food, provided by well-wishers.

Over the months that followed, Paddy's initiative took a more enduring form. His approach to Sir Keith Joseph paid off. The Minister had already accepted Jim Horne's invitation to go out on the soup run, and although Sir

Keith's tenure soon came to an end with the 1974 General Election and the change of Government, his successor, Barbara Castle, responded just as warmly, endorsing the negotiations that had taken place between GLC officers and the Department of Health and Social Security.[4]

In a matter of weeks, St Mungo became the foremost organisation in London concerned with single homelessness. Down at the Marmite factory, St Mungo was occupying a three-storeyed building with 28,000 feet of accommodation. The GLC was funding any emergency repair work that had to be done and, depending upon the weather, as many as 300 people a night were now being provided with beds and food. This was all being done with the co-operation of government departments. Civil servants from the Department of Health and Social Security and the local Labour Exchange called there twice weekly. Nearby, O'Connor had found another group of properties, Lennox Buildings. This was a neatly arranged complex of forty flats and five cottages that had until recently been used by Lambeth Council as halfway house accommodation for homeless families. Lambeth had handed the properties back to the GLC which intended to demolish them and use the site as part of a major road scheme. They were badly vandalised, but no firm date had been set for the road scheme so Paddy O'Connor intervened, stopped the demolition, and had these properties handed over to St Mungo as well. Down in Battersea High Street, the Trust was also offered the temporary use of an old warehouse that was in the charge of the Housing Development Committee, and was also due for eventual demolition as part of the Althorpe Grove housing scheme.

---

[4] The Single Homeless Subcommittee of the GLC Housing Development Committee was formally established on 11 February 1974. This gave Paddy O'Connor some authority; previously he had had none. As its chairman he made personal approaches to Mrs Castle. Her subsequent reply, detailing the basis upon which the GLC would be allowed to use the Charing Cross Hospital, is contained in Appendix A. These terms were later modified in some minor details, and the building itself was subsequently sold to the Metropolitan Police (see p. 73).

And now there was Charing Cross. By any normal stretch of the imagination, St Mungo was taking on more than it could handle – but Paddy O'Connor didn't think so, and neither did Jim Horne. Their enthusiasm was boundless; what they lacked was the administration to handle such an enterprise. All their work was being done on a shoestring. Had it been left at that, with proper co-ordination and the introduction of an effective management, this exercise might have been hailed as a great success – but it wasn't.

By now Paddy O'Connor's initiatives were attracting widespread publicity. He and Jim Horne were appearing on radio and television to explain their work. The Press were becoming interested. Every day homeless people were turning up on the doorstep; volunteers were arriving to help them, and some organisations which had been trying to tackle this problem for years were watching a little jealously as the newcomers took all the credit. There were constant complaints about it all. Some came from St Mungo neighbours (who possibly had justification for feeling peeved now that their peace was being disturbed). Many were voiced by the management of the Civil Service Stores, the Strand department store almost adjacent to the Charing Cross Hospital building, who complained of constant shoplifting by St Mungo residents. Others came in the form of anonymous letters and phone calls either from disgruntled former staff or volunteers, or from the growing army of London social workers who were keenly turning Homelessness into an industry riddled with trade union agreements and restrictive practices. What had begun as a kind-hearted gesture by a Catholic socialist with old ideals turned into a maelstrom of rumour and twisted emotion in which no one knew what to believe.

Now that he had a small administration to support him, with a staff equivalent of about six Council officers, a personal assistant to organise his schedule and that

Council car to take him wherever he felt he needed to go, Paddy O'Connor began pushing the boundaries of his Single Homeless Committee's work still further, gathering around him a group of people whom he was convinced were as keen as he was to provide help for London's homeless. They mostly had one thing in common, a criminal past, but that didn't bother Paddy who believed (and told me) that the best work in this field would be done by those who had lived in the gutters themselves and knew what it was like to be down-and-out. Some may say this was naive, and even more (with the gift of hindsight) might share such an opinion, but it has to be said that Paddy O'Connor made no attempt to persuade anyone that he was leading a band of angels. Indeed, he did the very opposite, letting us all know of their criminal convictions; telling us that these were the people who would solve the problem because they had dossed on the Embankment themselves and had battled back to their feet after terms of imprisonment, and that we couldn't understand their strengths of character because we were all (and this included his Labour colleagues) 'just a bunch of fucking Tories'. Perhaps it was our fault that we gave him too much rope.

Whatever the blame (and mine is acknowledged), matters did get out of hand, although hundreds of people were provided with accommodation who otherwise might not have been, and the foundation was laid for today's programme of hostel provision in inner London. In such circumstances, blame is a difficult word to define – and there were many who believed (and still do) that Paddy O'Connor was a genuine pioneer. Jock Stallard, the Labour Member of Parliament for St Pancras North, told the House of Commons in May 1974:

> Many of us have been heartened by the attempts recently made by the Greater London Council on the initiative of Alderman Paddy O'Connor to do something about one of our most serious problems – that of the real homeless, the down-

and-outs, the drop-outs, and in many cases students and others who nightly sleep rough because there is no alternative. I want to pay tribute to what Paddy O'Connor and his GLC comrades have done in this respect.

The weakness lay in the lack of supervision and a failure to ensure the proper management of the expenditure of public funds. Looking back now, it is easy to see where the programme started to fall apart; this all began with the problems of another registered charity called Ladyeholme, which was run by an elderly lady, Miss Edith Laura Urch, who had spent much of her life helping homeless people.

This work had begun in 1952 when she founded Ladyeholme from her own home in Battersea, and, as the *Church of England Newspaper* put it, 'took people in difficult circumstances and used her Christian commitment and nursing training to care for them'. In 1958, she formally registered the charity, with a friend, Dillon McCarthy, as chairman, using four properties to resettle homeless people. In the years that followed, private individuals and local councils made other property available to her, and by 1972 Ladyeholme had about 100 units of accommodation, and was able to house up to 140 families at any one time, with some staying for as long as eighteen months.[5]

After the death of Mr McCarthy, Miss Urch invited Paddy O'Connor to become Chairman of Ladyeholme, and he, in turn, introduced her to one of his new-found colleagues, Douglas Curtis, who was later described in the *Daily Express* as 'an ex-convict with several convictions as a small time confidence trickster (who) held an economics degree from Cambridge'. Curtis and two other men, who both had criminal convictions, became involved

---

[5] This section of the narrative is based on letters written by Miss Urch to the author at the time, on audited accounts and other documents which she supplied, including press cuttings from the *Church of England Newspaper* (18 March 1977) and from the *Daily Express* (8 March 1977).

in running the charity, and early in 1975 they accused the then Treasurer of Ladyeholme of misappropriating funds of £6,000. Curtis took this information to Paddy O'Connor, who called in the police. Detectives made enquiries. A report was sent to the Director of Public Prosecutions, but no further legal action followed. The police later said that this was a civil matter.

Miss Urch's explanation was much more simple. She told the *Church of England Newspaper*:

> Without any warning or invitation from me, Mr Curtis brought along several of his ex-prison companions who asked me to give them money to repair houses. I did give them money but soon found that the work was either done very badly or not done at all.
>
> They collected rents from our tenants but did not pay the full amount over to Ladyeholme. They then took the best flats for their own use and refused to pay any rent or rates for them and Ladyeholme began to get into serious financial difficulties.

Whatever the truth of the matter (and Miss Urch's explanation does have a ring of honesty about it), Ladyeholme was heading for disaster. Her Honorary Treasurer had gone back to India. Large sums of money were owing to various suppliers and a court action had been started in Liverpool to wind up Ladyeholme because it had not paid hire purchase rentals for some equipment. The officers advising Paddy O'Connor felt that action had to be taken by the GLC because Ladyeholme was occupying twenty-seven of its short-life properties. Paddy O'Connor recommended that these properties should be transferred to a newly formed housing charity called Second Genesis, which had been set up by Douglas Curtis. When the matter came before the GLC's committee, it was explained that Curtis did have a criminal record, but had now 'gone straight', having passed to Cambridge where he had graduated with that economics degree, subsequently writing a book titled *From Dartmoor to Cambridge*. Furthermore, Paddy O'Connor insisted that it was Curtis who had suggested calling in the police – and so he must be above suspicion!

Not for the last time, no one knew what to believe. Miss Urch herself was adamant. She had spent twenty-five years of her life helping people with problems, prostitutes, single mothers with children and homeless families – and here she was, having all her properties taken away from her, including some she had bought herself with her own savings. 'In spite of everything and contrary to any logic, I and others believe this is God's work and as such will continue,' she told the *Church of England Newspaper*.

Within a matter of months, Second Genesis itself was to collapse in ruins, amid allegations of fraud and harassment. Meanwhile, Paddy O'Connor himself had become involved in yet another organisation that said it wanted to help him in his work for the homeless. This was NOVO, the National Organisation of Victims and Offenders, which formed itself into the NOVO Housing Association Ltd. Its founder and driving force was Adi Behram Irani, a highly articulate and well-spoken Indian immigrant, who also made no secret of his criminal past. He had twice been convicted for living off immoral earnings, and had also served terms for other offences. Like Curtis, he had been in Dartmoor, and had become involved with various prisoners' aid organisations before forming NOVO. And when Second Genesis ran into trouble, Paddy O'Connor recommended that the properties at the heart of the affair should now be transferred to NOVO.

And there we have the story in a nutshell. Miss Urch had lost her tiny empire. Her properties went first to Second Genesis, and then these and more were transferred to NOVO – the whole exercise being funded through this small annual budget of £50,000 allocated to the GLC

Single Homeless Committee, to include all their work and that of St Mungo. Any works of repair or maintenance had to be funded from that, and as the years passed (and we are talking only of the years 1974–6) more and more of the funds earmarked for St Mungo were actually switched, quite legally and with proper authorisation, to these other two organisations. On each occasion, the expenditure was authorised by a Committee document signed by the appropriately qualified Council officers, who verified that the various plumbing and other building works had been done, and then countersigned by Paddy O'Connor as Chairman of the Committee.

But this was only the tip of an iceberg. Possession of all these properties by St Mungo, Second Genesis and NOVO meant that maybe as many as 800, perhaps 1,000, people could now be provided with accommodation every night. The total number of beds made available was never precisely calculated, because possession of the properties was constantly changing and so was the nature of their occupation, with sometimes fifteen or twenty people being found beds in just one small house. This was not thought unusual because the whole point of the exercise was to provide some temporary anchor for the thousands of people who were roofless and wandering the streets with no other means of support. However, it could be seen later that the weakness of the whole operation lay in the fact that all those beds *may* have been available, without anyone knowing for sure how many were occupied – and this was crucial because each person with a settled address became eligible for DHSS benefit. These payments were made in the form of GIRO cheques which could be cashed in any Post Office with only minimal verification. The possibilities for fraud were enormous.

Chapter 4

Paddy O'Connor's world started to crumble late in 1975. By then he was so totally involved with the three different organisations that formed the central thrust of his initiative that it was difficult to distinguish between them. He and his assistant, Ann Clark, were both members of the boards of directors of NOVO and Second Genesis. The degree to which the two bodies overlapped was never known, and is now irrelevant, but it was clear that both they and St Mungo were catering for the same group of homeless people and that there was some degree of contact between them. Properties had been switched from Second Genesis to NOVO. Parts of the Marmite factory were occupied by NOVO, and St Mungo regularly referred homeless people to NOVO from Charing Cross.[1]

The first indications that all was not well came in the Shoreditch County Court when a Second Genesis tenant won an action for damages after alleging harassment, and this was followed by newspaper reports, in October and November 1975, in local East End weekly papers and later in the *Daily Mirror*, making allegations of harassment against NOVO. It was also reported that the Registrar of Friendly Societies had said NOVO would be prosecuted if it did not produce audited accounts.

Both organisations had been allocated properties in Tower Hamlets and, almost inevitably, had become embroiled with the local squatters' organisations. The squatters alleged that Second Genesis was charging excessive rents, which they undoubtedly were in comparison with the squatters, who were paying no rent at all, and regarded the very principle of property owner-

[1] Although the three organisations were the main beneficiaries of the GLC Single Homeless Committee, there were others. It was the accepted Council policy to find some short-term use for any building rather than leave it standing empty. See Appendix A.

ship and payment of rent as 'capitalist exploitation'.
Being well used to extracting political nuggets from situations like this, the squatters drew attention to the fact
that Second Genesis was not registered with the National
Federation of Housing Associations, the Charity Commission or the Housing Corporation. When the squatters'
allegations were put to Douglas Curtis, he described them
as 'complete lies from a bunch of middle-class layabouts
. . . there are a small group of squatters, well organised
and well educated, but few of them work. They use the
law to their own advantage and to prevent us taking over
properties to rehouse genuine homeless people.'[2]

As so often in this sorry tale, there was truth on all
sides. The squatters were middle class. They were well
educated. Few of them worked, and instead they spent
their daytime hours running their own offices, dis-
tributing literature to people who wanted to squat,
organising what was in effect a free legal advice service,
and maintaining a highly effective bush telegraph
system with 'friends' in both GLC and individual borough
housing departments. By this time there were over 5,000
people squatting in the inner areas of London, and their
service was so well co-ordinated that tenants moving
house would often find squatters waiting on their doorstep as they moved out of a dwelling – or already in
possession of the one they were moving to. It was clear
that Housing Department staff were providing squatters
with addresses of properties that were becoming available for allocation to help them jump the queue. In these
conditions of near-anarchy, where the hand that helped
always bore the deepest teeth-marks, NOVO, Second
Genesis and St Mungo were now cast as agents of the
GLC, standing in the way of the squatters' attempts to
help the homeless, and there was sometimes violence as
people fought with fists and weapons to take possession of

---

[2] See the story 'Association Accused of Harassment' in the *East London
Advertiser*, 12 February 1976.

individual properties.[3] These shenanigans spilled over into Labour Party politics as individual squatters began joining local Labour branches, serving on constituency management committees, and standing for elected office. Housing was their big issue. Whenever a major housing policy paper came before the GLC, or one of the key inner London boroughs, large demonstrations took place; as many as 200 squatters would suddenly appear,[4] and proceedings would be brought to a standstill while the police were called to clear the public galleries.

There is probably no word in the English language to describe adequately the political agitation that then existed on London's streets; all of which coincided with that period in the life of the Labour Government when there were constant strikes in the public undertakings, secondary banks going into liquidation, shares collapsing in value, and the £ being devalued. Mrs Thatcher was not alone in predicting economic and social ruin, and here, in microcosm, was one man's initiative, partially torn apart by the forces of the time, and also degenerating through its own inherent weakness.

Events were to prove that the squatters were right. There was something wrong with both NOVO and Second Genesis, and St Mungo needed different management. But (and I have tried throughout to show all aspects of the issue) the fact also remained that properties that otherwise would have stood empty were now being utilised, and certainly 800 and possibly 1,000 people were being provided with accommodation every night for a total outlay of public funds that lay well within the budgeted £50,000 a year.

That was the positive side of his achievement, but Paddy O'Connor must have known in his bones that his world was falling apart. He started drinking heavily, and

[3] There were several such battles when properties were let in Belhaven Street, Tower Hamlets.

[4] On one memorable occasion the author was the target for a bag of flour thrown from the GLC public gallery. It missed.

by midday when he came into the County Hall bar his hands would be shaking and a whisky-sweat covered his brow. Sometimes he had the shakes. One morning we were due to meet formally and our meeting was rearranged three times during the day by intermediaries until, eventually, two of his colleagues came round to my room and confided that Paddy was now unconscious, and had been carried out of the building on a stretcher. The stress was more than he could bear. To their credit, the Labour leadership made no secret of his problems. All the documentation concerning the shortcomings of NOVO and Second Genesis were shown to me, and it was agreed by Sir Horace Cutler (then Leader of the GLC Conservatives) and myself that we would not make a public issue of the affair, but would instead co-operate with the Labour administration in putting Paddy's programme back on course. It was agreed that Paddy's decisions would be subject to exceptional scrutiny; that he and his assistant Ann Clark would resign from NOVO and Second Genesis; that no more properties would be allocated to Second Genesis; and that the work of the three organisations would be strictly monitored with regular written reports thereon.

What none of us knew was that the squatters down in the East End of London now saw this whole affair in a very different light. They believed that these obliquely drafted committee documents concealed a public scandal, and passed on their information to the Yorkshire Television production team that had produced the highly acclaimed documentary *Johnny Go Home* (1975), exposing the activities of 'Bishop' Roger Gleaves and the London rent-boy racket. While we were all calmly trying to get Paddy's programme back on track without making anyone homeless, their researchers were eagerly sifting through all the GLC documents, visiting the different properties, and interviewing residents. Although they uncovered little that was not known, and made a few errors of their own along the way, the resulting TV programme, *Goodbye Longfellow Road*, proved devastating, coming as it did eight weeks before the 1977 GLC elections.

As is usually the case, whether in local authorities or national government, the party in power heard of Yorkshire TV's intended programme before anyone else did. The Council staff, operating within the same broad conventions as the civil service, briefed Sir Reg Goodwin and his colleagues on the enquiries they had been receiving. Richard Balfe, now a member of the European Parliament and then Chairman of the GLC Housing Development Committee, demanded action. He said he wanted to see a script for the programme in advance, and there were suggestion in the Press that if this were not provided the GLC would either ask the Independent Broadcasting Authority to intervene, or would institute High Court proceedings to block the programme. Nothing could have given Yorkshire TV better advance publicity; the moves to ban *Goodbye Longfellow Road* became the front-page lead story in the London evening newspapers before the programme had even been shown. A special advance screening was arranged for the London Press, and Paddy O'Connor guaranteed Yorkshire TV even more publicity by turning up for this uninvited – and then being denied entry. He was photographed in the London *Evening Standard* giving Yorkshire TV his V-sign, describing them as 'a load of bums'.

Goodbye Longfellow Road was shown on 8 March 1977, provoking immediate national uproar, with front-page headlines and full-page features in the national Press, Questions in Parliament, statements by Ministers, and – since the GLC election campaign was just beginning – the story ran and ran. Politically, the programme was a gift for the Conservative Party and one that its candidates exploited to the full. My own comment that Paddy O'Connor had merely allowed his heart to rule his head brought demands for my resignation. Didn't I recognise corruption when it stared me in the face? Didn't I know that the time to put the boot in was when your opponent was on the ground? Paddy's reaction to that comment was characteristic of the man. 'What the fucking hell's a heart for if it doesn't rule your head?' said he when we met in a GLC corridor.

The allegations that he had to answer were serious. There was a clear implication of corruption, and it was stated boldly that NOVO and Second Genesis had used properties acquired from the GLC to exploit the homeless. Graphic film was shown of families living in miserable conditions. Bailiffs were shown arriving to evict one family. Another family, a mother with two young children, was shown living in squalor. It was suggested that another family had been forced to leave their home at night after living there for over seventy years. And it was suggested that none of this would have been possible without the £19,000 allocated by the GLC to Second Genesis and the £40,000 to NOVO for the renovation of these properties. Nancy Banks-Smith, television critic of *The Guardian*, commented:

GOODBYE LONGFELLOW ROAD

The most important thing about television, so vital that like air you don't notice it, is that it happens in your home. There is singing in the street when the pub turns out. A fire engine or ambulance screams past. The door bell or telephone rings. The world is out there but it's not coming in and you're not going out.

In living memory which means mine, the programmes which suck you to the set, like Goldfinger to the plane window, are about homelessness. Cathy Come Home, Johnnie Go Home and Goodbye Longfellow Road.

The last two are documentaries by Yorkshire but by the same formidable team. When Michael Deakin, head of documentaries, was talking about Johnnie on radio a man brought a cardboard suitcase to him with much of the evidence contained in Goodbye Longfellow Road. They were crying scandals only needing someone to listen.

For a year. It took John Willis's team a year of their time and Yorkshire's money.

Longfellow Road is a dying street in Tower Hamlets, designated as a slum for 50 years, for demolition for more than 30. Rejuvenated by a strong transfusion of young squatters, many of them doctors and teachers who work in the area but can find nowhere to live. Efficient, articulate and outlandish. 'Worse than the coloureds,' to the oldest inhabitants. 'They want to clean their windows,' said 82-year-old Alice Morter censoriously. 'What they are doing indoor all day, Gawd only knows. They want to come out into the air.'

Alice Morter and her husband James, with one of those sacrificial daughters, Louise, have lived in the street since 1916 and have had their bags packed to go since 1974. Someone had forgotten about them. When they moved at last, in the dark of the evening, looking doubtfully over the hearthdoor at their removal van like horses going to the knackers, she was crying and he was dying.

Six weeks after they moved into their nice, bright flat – 'Look mam, a loo. How long since you sat on one of them?' – James Morter was dead.

Irene Thompson, thin as a broom with two baby daughters, a gruff little voice and blitz humour. 'Lost the health lady thou'n that,' she growled, stepping round the hole in the floor on the way to the outside loo. 'Do you really want to look inside?' she asked doubtfully, shoving at the door. The shattered lavatory and the black beetles shoved back.

When the rain reached the electricity, there was a flash, the cry of a child, and she was living in a damp, dark, lethal dump. After 16 days of council promises and hope deferred, she was taken away with pneumonia. 'The housing conditions are the main cause of her illness,' said the doctor. 'She comes from an East End culture where the idea of her children going into care is anathema but nobody should be living here.'

That house was one of 35 the GLC's Housing Subcommittee headed by Alderman Paddy O'Connor gave to a housing association called Second Genesis with £19,000 for their improvement. Novo, another such association, had 21 houses and £40,000. The idea was to provide safe, decent shells for the totally homeless.

Both Douglas Curtis, the founder of Second Genesis, and Adi Rani of Novo were said to be ex-Dartmoor prisoners with wide experience ranging from false pretences and fraud to possession of weapons with ammunition and living on immoral earnings.

Goodbye Longfellow Road peppered the screen with fact and figures about misappropriated funds as if, like Sherlock Holmes, it was writing its names in bullets. Statistics however lethal are extremely hard to take off a screen. It is like catching bullets by hand but the evidence of a heartless racket in homelessness and the consistent warm support of Alderman O'Connor ('I will support them to the hilt as long as I can') are such that one cannot doubt the final destination of those bullets.

When Michael Deakin called by arrangement at the GLC's desirable residence on the South bank to check several questions eventually asked in the programme he was evicted.

Which, in the circumstances, is both neat and appropriate.

There were front-page lead stories in *The Daily Telegraph*, the *Daily Express*, the *Evening News*, the *Evening Standard* and the *Daily Mirror*, over a period of several days, with trenchant editorials, extensive coverage in other national papers, bulletins in all the TV and radio news programmes, and a constant barrage of criticism within Parliament. It was a crucial moment in the history of London government, coming as it did when there was still time for it to become a major issue in the GLC election campaign. There were widespread demands for the abolition of the GLC. Twenty-seven Independent candidates stood on the Abolition ticket, and although none was successful pressure for the Council's abolition intensified from that moment on.

The Council's Chief Officers, the Director General (Sir James Swaffield), the Comptroller of Financial Services (Maurice Stonefrost) and the Controller of Housing (Harry Simpson), were alert to these implications and, unusually for professionally independent administrators in a pre-election period, signed a Council report justifying much of the Single Homeless Committee's programme. Their statement, which is reproduced in full in Appendix B, endeavoured to put *Goodbye Longfellow Road* in the wider context of all that had been done in conjunction with St Mungo and other charities to alleviate London's homelessness. But it was too late. The damage had been done.

For Paddy O'Connor himself, the consequences were devastating. He was suffering from double pneumonia, having been out on the soup run during cold wet winter nights, and was literally assailed on his sick bed and accused of being a party to the corruption and exploitation of the very people he had been endeavouring to help. As might be expected of the man, his response was rugged.

Hugh Rossi, the Conservative MP for Hornsey and the Party's Housing spokesman, said *Goodbye Longfellow Road* was 'very disturbing. There was evidence that more than negligence was involved. The whole thing reeked of corruption.' Geoffrey Finsberg, the Conservative MP for Hampstead, added that there had been 'clear evidence of maladministration'. The Attorney General said there was going to be a police investigation. And, in perhaps the unkindest rub of all, the squatters' leader Piers Corbyn, who was becoming an influential figure in the London Labour movement, said *Goodbye Longfellow Road* had shown that it is not the action of the homeless – but the policies of housing authorities and corrupt housing associations which cause the housing crisis. In the light of these facts it is deplorable that the Government is trying to criminalise squatting and all forms of occupation. In fact, squatting is the only answer to the housing problems of 40,000 people in Britain. We demand prosecution for those who attack the homeless.

To every allegation, Paddy O'Connor had but one reply. 'I am not a crook,' he said. 'For God's sake, my budget is only £50,000 a year. What can you waste with that? My job is to find a roof for homeless people, to get them off the streets, and that is what we do ... I have not been foolhardy with the ratepayers' money. I may have been foolish and misguided many times in my life, but not about this ... I've nothing to hide. I'm too old to be naive.'

In an interview with the *News of the World*, he defended himself vigorously, saying:

> I'm a drinker and a lecher – but I'm no crook. My hands are clean and my conscience is clear ... I understand what the implications are, that money in council grants has been going into my own pocket. But there isn't a word of truth in it. If there were I'd have resigned by now. But I'm damned if I'm going to. I looked closely at these people's credentials. But must we condemn people for life because they have been convicted? Are you going to say to someone, 'Because you've been a crook, you'll always be a crook'? I am convinced that they are doing a good job and are not dishonest. My judgement has been called into question but I'm prepared to stand by them ... I've no regrets at all. I've had a good life. I've done everything I ever wanted to do. I may have mostly done it all the wrong way, but at least I've done it.

Sir Reg Goodwin and Richard Balfe stood by him, with Goodwin saying: 'Paddy O'Connor still has my full confidence. He has done a heroic and magnificent job which few people would have been prepared to tackle. He has found some means through the Council machine of helping people who would otherwise have slept on the Embankment and maybe died of exposure.' Balfe commented: 'A number of people would have been dead today but for the quite selfless work that Paddy O'Connor put in.'

But it was too late to save him. On 23 March, the Kensington Labour Party dropped O'Connor as their candidate for the GLC elections by 29 votes to 26, with one abstention. 'Had he pleaded with us he might have helped himself,' said one member afterwards. O'Connor himself told *The Daily Telegraph*, 'I am obviously unhappy. I told the committee I am not a crook and have never been crooked. I was not prepared to say that NOVO was a bunch of crooks.' This was the end of his career, and his programme of work for the single homeless lay in tatters.

Chapter 5

Events often turn on minor issues. Time and again wars have been fought and campaigns waged to avenge some small offence, and so it is with domestic affairs as well. Government policies frequently change, not for reasons of deep philosophical argument or as a result of statistical analysis but because someone somewhere does something that upsets the political applecart. Although he never knew it, Paddy O'Connor did that – and the furore surrounding *Goodbye Longfellow Road* prompted an important change in British housing policy.

Stripped of all its drama, the Yorkshire TV documentary had one central point. Why was public money being spent on this new social policy without proper safeguards? With power changing hands at County Hall in the days after the GLC elections, and Paddy O'Connor's life in ruins, the Press soon lost interest. They had had their crucifixion, and that was that, but within Whitehall and in Parliament the politicians became interested in the wider ramifications of the whole affair. With the Housing (Homeless Persons) Bill travelling through the House of Commons, there were questions to be answered, and mileage to be had.

Why was the GLC working with housing associations when the Housing Corporation had been set up by Parliament to do just that? Had the GLC exceeded its powers? Why hadn't the Housing Corporation used the additional powers given to it by the 1974 Housing Act to bring this situation under control?

NOVO and Second Genesis soon disappeared from the public stage. Months before *Goodbye Longfellow Road* had been screened, Second Genesis had already run into trouble and its properties had been transferred to NOVO. Second Genesis was now being wound up, and one of its directors was said to have been in a Belgian gaol. The GLC decided to repossess the NOVO properties, and although some of its residents put up a spirited resistance in the courts, eventually did just that. All those police enquiries led nowhere. There were no prosecutions, but those underlying questions still remained to be answered, and there was still the problem of St Mungo, which was providing a similar service for the single homeless from the Charing Cross Hospital buildings, Lennox Buildings, the Marmite factories and other individual houses that had been allocated by the GLC. Was its relationship with the GLC doubtful too?

Initially, officials of the Housing Corporation had told the Press that they had never been approached by Paddy O'Connor or officials of the GLC about these schemes to help the single homeless, adding that if they had been 'it was extremely likely that they would have been turned down' (*The Daily Telegraph*, 10 March 1977). Conservative politicians making enquiries into the Corporation's attitude found they had been reluctant to tackle single homelessness, which was regarded as 'difficult' and a matter for welfare authorities and not housing. If that was the case, it was said, why not abolish the Housing Corporation and replace it with something more sensitive, or, at the very least, sack its chairman and chief officers?[1]

Under these pressures, with a General Election approaching, the Corporation's attitude began to change. Housing associations anxious to help clients with 'special needs' were soon told they would become eligible for Corporation funding. Then, in 1980, a special allocation

---

[1] The Housing Corporation had been the brainchild of Sir Keith Joseph and his Permanent Under Secretary at the then Ministry of Housing and Local Government, the late Dame Evelyn Sharpe. It came into being with the enactment of the 1964 Housing Act. The appointment of the first Chairman was a matter of some hilarity. He was recently retired Admiral of the Fleet Sir Caspar John. The Liberal Leader Jo Grimond commented, 'You might as well put an architect in charge of the Navy.'

of £12,000,000 was announced, and those organisations that had been the pioneers in this field were advised that if they chose to register as housing associations they, too, would become eligible for sufficient public funds to do their work effectively. It was all too good to be true.

Until this moment, registration with the Housing Corporation had not been a prerequirement for GLC funding. There were many organisations that called themselves 'housing associations' that had never bothered to register with the Corporation, and there was no necessity for them to do so. In the late sixties, in the early days of the Corporation's life, the GLC had introduced the principle of 'third sector funding', setting aside £20,000,000 a year for housing association developments. Within the GLC, the Housing Corporation was regarded as a newcomer to London politics of somewhat doubtful parentage.

Those GLC officers who had spent their working lives as servants of the old London County Council, under the leadership of Herbert Morrison and Ike Hayward, gave the Corporation barely a glance and implemented the 'third sector' programme, never thinking for a moment that the associations with which they dealt ought to register with the Corporation. Within this overall policy, the part played by Paddy O'Connor and his Single Homeless Subcommittee was very small beer. They handled fifty-six properties out of a total GLC allocation to the 'third sector' of over 2,000 dwellings. These fifty-six included all the properties handled by Second Genesis, NOVO and St Mungo.

As the *Goodbye Longfellow Road* furore rumbled on, the Housing Corporation tune was changing. They were now anxious to be seen helping the single homeless and St Mungo, which had formed a housing association to take advantage of the provisions of the 1974 Housing Act, was now advised to turn to the Corporation for funding.

By then, Jim Horne had been running St Mungo for eight years. The whole project was largely his creation, and he had gathered around him a team of paid workers and a group of volunteers, some of whom served upon his management committee. There had been occasional ruptures, with staff being either dismissed or resigning (sometimes en bloc), but this has never been unusual in the voluntary sector. The emotional commitment is such that passions tend to run high, and there is a natural tension built into the system between the 'workers', who depend upon the sector for their livelihoods, and the 'volunteers', who earn their living elsewhere.

Jim Horne had managed to balance these interests with some success, and had at the same time attracted widespread support for St Mungo from government and civil servants, from GLC members and staff, from some City trusts and businessmen, and the Press. Earl Mountbatten had been helpful from the start. Heinz had supplied food and soup almost since the beginning of the soup run. Horne's style was rough and ready. Some might call it tough. One member of the staff was sacked for stealing from a rubbish skip a kitchen cabinet with a broken back and no doors and a few boards that had been used for shelving. She had taken her case to an Industrial Tribunal, which decided that Horne had acted harshly and unreasonably and ordered that St Mungo pay her £1,300 compensation.[2] The case had been supported by her union, the Transport and General Workers, who had complained to the Advisory Conciliation and Arbitration Service that St Mungo refused to recognise it. In its evidence to the tribunal, the union had said that some of St Mungo's fifty full-time 'workers' were paid only £3–4 a week plus their board and lodging, and in giving its adjudication the court stated that the items alleged to have been stolen were 'virtually valueless'. The case was described as trivial, and the tribunal added: 'We prefer the evidence of the applicant, whom we accept as a

[2] See report headed '£1,300 for "Harshly" Sacked Charity Girl', *Evening Standard*, 11 November 1976.

witness of truth, to that of Mr Horne, whose evidence we
consider to be unreliable.'

This intervention by the Transport and General
Workers Union coincided with a recruiting drive
throughout the voluntary sector by different trade
unions. It was fertile ground. The sector was growing
with the expansion of the Housing Corporation, the emer-
gence of several major housing associations (as a result of
amalgamations and large building programmes), and the
formation of advice agencies, research bodies and other
charities concerned with homelessness. Many started in a
small way and had never been able to pay large salaries.
Some had developed along the Simon Community principle that high wages were wrong in any case, and within
this expanding field there were many conflicting philosophies, including the idea that all managerial decisions
should be taken collectively by 'the workers'. This was an
idea that had many supporters. Some agencies did
become workers' collectives, but Jim Horne was among
those who asserted the traditional view that 'management must be free to manage'. This was a source of
conflict within St Mungo, which became overmagnified in
times of crisis – and these were frequent because St
Mungo was spread over different buildings and was
always short of money. It was a situation that was bound
to breed factions within St Mungo, and it did.

By then St Mungo had the following projects under its
wing:

The Marmite Factory

These large factory premises in Durham Street, Kennington, had been in poor repair when St Mungo first
moved there, in December 1973, to run that first Christmas emergency shelter. Occupation had always been on a
temporary basis, with St Mungo paying no rent and

agreeing to surrender the premises as soon as they were needed for redevelopment. The GLC had made small sums available to St Mungo for emergency repairs, and had also funded those repairs to the sewage system in 1974 (see p. 34), but the local planning authority, Lambeth Council, had never been happy with the situation and the occupation had only continued because the GLC had backed St Mungo, and had suggested that it would, if necessary, invoke its own planning powers which overrode those of the borough council. All the parties agreed that the premises were unsuitable for hostel use. The building comprised a basement and two further floors, totalling 28,000 square feet, and was too large and too dilapidated for adaptation. The hostel use continued on this temporary basis for more than five years, with St Mungo accommodating between ninety and 300 people a night, depending upon the season and the weather. Beds and blankets were provided with breakfast plus soup in the evenings. This basic service only ended in 1979 with the opening of the Bondway hostel near Vauxhall Bridge as an alternative to Marmite.

Charing Cross Hospital

The occupation of these premises had always been a tangled affair. Originally, the DHSS had agreed that the GLC could acquire and then allocate to St Mungo the right to occupy the building. The wording was left as vague as that because 'ownership' was at one time believed to lie with the North-West Thames Regional Health Authority, and then later it was discovered that an original building lease dating back to 1840 empowered the Crown Commissioners to buy the freehold back at a fair market value, if at any time the building ceased to be a hospital. Different parts of the building

were occupied by other charities, but the main occupant
was St Mungo and its full potential was about 500 beds –
although undertakings were given that no more than 150
homeless people would be accommodated at any one
time.[3]

Throughout St Mungo's occupation, there were crises of
different kinds. Local traders, particularly the management of the Civil Service Stores, objected strongly to the
presence of so many destitute and shabby-looking people
near their premises, complaining that it brought down
the 'tone' of the area, and that there was constant shoplifting.

Another problem was that when the residents had
received their weekly money from the DHSS, word would
soon get round, and prostitutes would slip into the building to service the men, moving from bed to bed.

Originally, it had been hoped that the Charing Cross
hostel would become a permanent project – but those
hopes ended with the discovery of that 1840 building
lease. Then there were financial crises in running the
project and internal divisions between the staff, all of this
overshadowed by the constant threat of closure. Eighteen
months before that Industrial Tribunal case, there had
been other complaints about Jim Horne's management
by members of the staff, and the GLC officers responsible
for overseeing the project had publicly reported to one of
its committees:

> At first the standard of management achieved and the pro-
> gress made by St Mungo was very encouraging. In recent
> months, however, there has been some cause for concern
> about management standards, particularly as regards the
> quality of the meals service and amount spent on food; the
> comparatively slow increase in numbers of residents and

---

[3] Those undertakings were often broken; it was the policy not to turn
homeless people away, and there were enough beds to accommodate up
to 550! This was not something that the planning authorities or fire
prevention officers were able to monitor because each night was
different.

relations with staff, rates of pay, retention, etc. A petition from two dissatisfied members of staff was received making allegations of serious deficiencies in St Mungo management and although these charges were subsequently withdrawn by the complainants, investigation showed that there had at least at one time been some substance in the complaints.

I have had discussions with Jim Horne, Director of the Trust, and other members of his staff and am satisfied that the assurances they have given provide a reasonable chance (though no absolute guarantee) that a standard will in future be achieved which, while by no means perfect, is reasonable in this difficult field which has been so neglected by more conventional and better established voluntary bodies; and that the standards will compare favourably with those achieved by the best of the newer, less orthodox, bodies which are the only ones engaged in this type of work.[4]

At that stage the GLC considered withdrawing from the operation altogether or handing it over to another organisation, but eventually resolved to continue working with St Mungo which had set up the St Mungo Community Housing Association Ltd. This had been established to benefit from the financial provisions of the 1974 Housing Act under which Housing Association Grants, Revenue Deficit Grants or Hostel Deficit Grants could be given to associations that were registered with the Housing Corporation. St Mungo had estimated that it was eligible for grants totalling £150,000 which would cover the estimated deficits on its operations, but the Housing Corporation was reluctant to make these monies available because of the uncertainties that surrounded St Mungo's occupation of the building.

Meanwhile, the GLC had agreed to make up to £100,000 available for essential building works (although not all of this was spent), and St Mungo was endeavouring to stabilise its position by formally apply-

4 Report to the GLC Single Homeless Committee by the Director of Housing Development and Construction, dated 19 May 1975.

ing for planning consent for the whole building to be used for hostel purposes. (This consent was never given.) Despite all these uncertainties, Charing Cross continued to provide shelter for at least 150 homeless people every night although its very existence was becoming a source of heated debate within London's housing movement, which was becoming increasingly trade union organised and politically led.

Lennox Buildings

This complex of some forty flats and five cottages had been allocated to St Mungo by the GLC on a short-term basis (see p. 36), and had now been partially renovated with the use of GLC funds totalling approximately £40,000. The complex was used to provide accommodation for as many as sixty to eighty homeless men who had mostly been referred there from Charing Cross.

In addition to this complex, St Mungo had also been allocated individual dwellings in Abercrombie Street, London SW11; Bravington Road, London W9; Alma Road, London SW18; Camberwell New Road, London SE6; Ebner Street, London SW18; Heber Road, London SE22; Rymer Road, London SE22; Rymer Road, London SW18 and Commercial Road, London E1, on a short-life basis and these were also being used to provide accommodation for the homeless.[5]

All told, the Marmite factory, Charing Cross, Lennox Buildings and these other properties enabled St Mungo to provide accommodation for as many as 700 to 800 people a night, which was more than any other voluntary agency had ever done (with the exception of the Salvation Army). It was an extraordinary achievement, and one that had

[5] It should be stated, in view of matters mentioned later in this book, that the GLC had no complaints over the management of its properties. St Mungo financed the maintenance themselves, and GLC officers reported that they usually paid the monthly charges (i.e. rent) promptly.

earned Jim Horne a reputation for cutting through red tape to get things done. He had the support of his committees and of officers within the Department of Health and Social Security, and there were suggestions being quietly made that the time had come to recommend him for an Honour.

It was then that the thunderbolts struck. First, he miscalculated the effects of that Industrial Tribunal. Horne had been used to riding his staff fairly hard and never expected to be roughed-up by the Tribunal (and that damaged his standing with the civil servants). Second, there was that *Goodbye Longfellow Road* TV programme which soured the atmosphere for every unconventional charity trying to help the single homeless. Third, there was the charged political climate with the Housing (Homeless Persons) Bill passing through Parliament and MPs asking why was the GLC funding St Mungo when the Housing Corporation had been set up to finance the voluntary movement, and why had the Corporation failed to police the movement effectively.

Opinions change swiftly in public life. Just a few years earlier Jim Horne had been in the right place at the right time to help many hundreds of homeless people. Now, events were conspiring against him.

Chapter 6

The whole of the Paddy O'Connor initiative came to a tragic end. With his removal from public life by the Kensington Labour Party, Paddy lost the will to live. He was a broken man.

Three years earlier he had had a heart attack and had been advised to drink less, smoke less, and change his diet. The advice had been ignored and he had thrown himself into his work for the single homeless, visiting hostels during the day and then spending some nights out on the soup run. During the early months of 1977 he had been out in the cold and the wet and had caught double pneumonia, and now there was the stress of *Goodbye Longfellow Road* and all the attendant publicity. It was too much for him.

During those months the lease on his flat came up for renewal. It was just a formality. He was entitled to a new lease but was so dispirited that he did not even answer the letter. In a state of acute depression he was admitted to a psychiatric ward of St Pancras Hospital, totally unable to cope with his problems. With his failure to answer that letter, his landlords exercised their right to repossession. Homelessness stared him in the face and he did not care. When the GLC Director of Housing, Len Bennett, went to see him in hospital and told him that another flat would be found for him, Paddy O'Connor burst into tears. He died six months later, aged 61.

Until the very end, Sir Reg Goodwin stood by him and so did the friends he had made through NOVO. Destitute men and women wearing rags stood side by side with black-suited Labour and Conservative politicians at his funeral. It was an intensely sad occasion.

During the last months of his life, Paddy O'Connor had avoided contact with his former colleagues, although he continued to support NOVO, who were now facing pressure from the GLC to close down their operations and hand back their properties to the Council. A local Hackney councillor, Sam Springer MBE, also supported both O'Connor and NOVO and helped the residents in their campaign to keep the hostel open. The hostel became known as 'Carmel's Commune' after the name of one of its residents, Mrs Carmel Carter, who led the fight to preserve the complex of buildings at 140–148 Lansdowne Drive, Hackney, and nearby 26 Ivydene Road, as one entity.[1] They were also supported by Anton Wallich-Clifford, founder of the Simon Community.

After all that had gone on before, the GLC saw the transfer of the NOVO properties to an association with a better reputation, and the reorganisation of St Mungo, as the essential steps that had to be taken if it were to continue supporting new initiatives to help the single homeless. The *Goodbye Longfellow Road* allegations, with their implicit charge of corruption, had made the whole exercise a minefield. Government departments, which are also run by men who have to protect their reputations, were being cautious. The Housing Corporation was at last beginning to flex the muscle given to it by the 1974 Housing Act. At private meetings with those responsible for GLC housing policy, the Secretary of State for the Environment, Peter Shore, and the Housing Minister, Reg Freeson, both agreed that they would support the GLC and the Housing Corporation in 'clearing up the mess'. Similar meetings were held with Professor David Donnison, Chairman of the Supplementary Benefits Commission, and Sir Lou Sherman, who

---

[1] This dispute between Carmel's Commune and the GLC continued for nearly three years, with various Court actions. It was eventually ended in January 1980 when the High Court gave the GLC an order for possession. There were then thirty-six residents. Mr Justice Caulfield praised Mrs Carter for her work and said she ran the premises with devotion, efficiency, honesty and compassion. 'She showed great abilities and did a remarkable job,' he said.

had been appointed Chairman of the Housing Corporation. There was general agreement between them all that the GLC would help to find properties and provide 'topping up finance' for the voluntary sector; that the Corporation would allocate substantial funds for new buildings and conversion schemes to meet 'special needs', and that the payment of benefits to those living in hostels would be streamlined to ensure the flow of revenue that was needed for their everyday expenses.

Although he had not lived to see it, the very objective that Paddy O'Connor had fought for was now being achieved; a change in national policy that would ensure a continuing flow of resources to organisations helping the single homeless so that they could be properly run and effectively managed. It was not a policy that could be immediately quantified, although the GLC increased its budget for single homelessness from £50,000 a year to £1m and the Housing Corporation, having committed itself to supporting 'special needs projects', went on to allocate £12m. A small department was established within the GLC Housing Department to deal specifically with the voluntary sector.

It was generally agreed that the first issue to be tackled was St Mungo. There had been those staff problems and budget deficits; complaints about the management, and even the quality of the food (for some strange reason, there were complaints about the gravy!), and its work had been undertaken in so many different buildings, which were all occupied on a temporary basis and contrary to the planning laws and general principles of public health legislation. It was agreed that the Housing Corporation would now take the lead in helping St Mungo sort out its affairs, but a problem quickly arose. When the lawyers started looking through the finer detail of the 1974 Housing Act, they thought that even these powers might be insufficient and Clauses were therefore drafted for the next Housing Bill which was already in preparation.[2]

Before any funds had been made available to St Mungo, the Housing Corporation launched an enquiry into St Mungo's affairs under Section 19 of the 1974 Housing Act, without any prior notification to the management committee.[3] This was soon followed by an enquiry by the Charity Commission under Section 6 of the Charities Act, and around the same time an employee/approached the Metropolitan Police and laid complaints against Jim Horne, alleging misuse of grant monies, misuse of vehicles and forgery of documents. This was a shattering sequence of events because St Mungo, as then constituted, was in no position to defend itself. The Trust and the Housing Association overlapped for reasons that were historical, as much as anything else – because the Trust had set up the Association. But now St Mungo's difficulties were compounded by confusion as to whether or not particular items of expenditure should have been spent by the Trust or the Association. The Committee had difficulty deciding whether there had been a muddle or something worse – and so did the police. Extensive enquiries were made into Jim Horne's personal background and into every aspect of St Mungo's affairs and, inevitably, in such a poisonous atmosphere, there were leaks, to *Labour Weekly* and *The Guardian*. Rumours spread quickly in October and November 1978. On 21 December a story appeared in the London *Evening Standard* headlined 'Charity Boss Says No Fear Of Probe.'

The situation was complex, against that long background of Paddy O'Connor's campaign, the *Goodbye*

[2] This is another curious tale. Much of this Bill was drafted while Peter Shore was Secretary of State. However, the 1979 General Election intervened – and so the incoming Conservative Government included these Clauses in what became their 1980 Housing Act.

[3] It should be stated, in fairness to the Corporation, that there were doubts expressed as to whether or not the Committee were controlling the Director. They thought they were and were understandably miffed.

Longfellow Road exposures and the furore in Parliament
and the Press, and it was difficult for Jim Horne to be
given a fair hearing – or for the Committee to make itself
heard. This was not a case of smoke without fire; there
was something smouldering away beneath it all – complaints that were genuine, and others that may have been
rooted in malice.

The Committee met regularly throughout October,
November, and December, and on 15 December three
members of the Committee (John Cornwell, John Ander-
son and Tim Maskell) met officials of the Housing Corporation, and Mr Rogers who was conducting the enquiry on
their behalf and also on behalf of the Charity Commission. At this meeting it was suggested that it 'did not
have sufficient control over the Director'. On 2 January
1979, the Chairman, John Cornwell, met Detective Chief
Superintendent Griggs of the Metropolitan Police and
was told of the suggestion that there might have been a
misuse of funds and forgery of documents. The Committee met again on 3 January, and a few days later was
advised that Jim Horne had been charged with various
criminal offences. At its next meeting on 12 January it
was agreed that his appointment as Director be suspended. The Committee members signed a document saying:

> The Trustees of the St Mungo Community Trust and the
> Management Committee of the St Mungo Housing Associ-
> ation Ltd have agreed, with effect from 12 January 1979, to
> Mr Jim Horne's request that he step down as Director of both
> the Trust and Housing Association until such time as he has
> an opportunity to answer the charges that have been made
> against him. Mr Jim Horne feels that such a course of action
> is in the best interests of the Trust, the Housing Association
> and himself.

At this same meeting, the Committee was advised by its
solicitor that if it did not take this action it was almost
certain that the Housing Corporation or the Charity Com-

mission would do so. He also went on to explain that either of these two bodies had the power to dismiss or suspend any or all members of the management committee.[4]

When the Director was suspended, the manager of St Mungo's small hostel project at Hammersmith, Ron Upton, was appointed to run Charing Cross on a temporary basis. St Mungo's affairs were temporarily run from Abercrombie Street in Westminster, where St Mungo was running a bail hostel. The Chairman, John Cornwell, was in hospital.

It was a time of great crisis in St Mungo's affairs. The Trustees had been hoping to receive substantial funds from the Housing Corporation. These were not sent, and St Mungo's bankers refused to meet some cheques. The Committee met again to consider closing down the Charing Cross Hospital and giving all members of staff notice of provisional redundancy. It was at this point, when morale was at its lowest, that the Housing Corporation insisted on using its powers under Section 20 of the

---

[4] Fourteen criminal charges were eventually laid against Jim Horne. The trial began at the Old Bailey on 21 October 1980, and Jim Horne strongly denied the charges. It eventually became clear that the police case against him was thin. The prosecution dropped thirteen of the charges. Horne then pleaded guilty to one charge of uttering a forged document. On 19 November he was sentenced to nine months in prison. The Court of Appeal set aside this sentence on 16 December and substituted a two-month sentence suspended for two years. Mr Justice Boreham, sitting with Lord Lane (the Lord Chief Justice) and Mr Justice Kenneth Jones said the case could not be completely overlooked, but to do justice to Mr Horne and society his sentence could be reduced and suspended. The Judge said that in 1977 the housing association had the use of the old Charing Cross Hospital building which it shared with the Trust. It was used as a hostel for single homeless men and students, but two areas were unfit for use . . . Mr Horne had paid workmen in cash for renovating these areas, and this money had come from rent received by the housing association. A £25,000 deficit was discovered in the association's rental income. At the Central Criminal Court, receipts were produced which proved that the money had gone to the builders. But it remained, the Judge said, that Mr Horne admitted during the investigation that he had produced a forged invoice. Mr Justice Boreham said the Court of Appeal was now satisfied that no substantial deficit was involved. See *The Times*, 17 December 1980.

1974 Housing Act to restructure the board of St Mungo's. Six new members of the board were appointed, three chosen by the Corporation and three from outside.[5]

The new board met for the first time on 5 February 1979 and was told that financial assistance would be forthcoming from the Housing Corporation for the St Mungo Community Housing Association Ltd, but that thereafter there would have to be a strict distinction between its activities and those of the St Mungo Community Trust. They would become two wholly separate organisations.

Under this arrangement, Charing Cross, the Marmite project and Lennox Buildings all remained with the Association – and the soup run stayed with the Trust, which also retained the bail hostel at Abercrombie Street and the hostel in Hammersmith.

It was not a happy divorce. Given all the circumstances, this was hardly surprising. Suspicions ran deep. If the Housing Corporation was being a bit too bullish or the GLC somewhat slow to respond, one had to understand that there was a general anxiety to be 'whiter than white' in all their dealings – and both were working closely with the Department of the Environment and the Supplementary Benefits Commission. One point was established from the start; none of the residents was going to be made homeless. But that was about the only point that was clear – and none of the parties felt able to tell the Committee of their intentions while the Director was still on suspension, facing criminal charges. The

---

[5] At that time, for reasons explained earlier, the Housing Corporation had little involvement in single homelessness. Its staff knew few people in this field. The author was invited to put forward three names for the new St Mungo board by the then Chairman of the Corporation, Sir Lou Sherman. The author nominated the Revd Austen Williams, Francis Bergin and Robert Greenshields, who were respectively Chairman, Treasurer and an Executive Committee member of the National Association of Voluntary Hostels. The other three nominees were Mrs Joan Forsyth and Mr Anthony T. Shephard, who were both Corporation employees, and Major William Bramwell-Baird of the Salvation Army.

original Committee was understandably hurt. The chairman, John Cornwell, felt the Section 19 enquiry was a reflection upon his character, and, being a solicitor by profession, found this deeply wounding. Some of the Committee still had confidence in Jim Horne and there was the additional problem which, as has been explained already, was characteristic of the homeless field at the time, that there were staff who believed that none of these problems would have happened had the organisation been differently run. Those beliefs were partly philosophical, but there had also been a serious clash of personalities between some staff and the Director.

In the months that followed, John Cornwell and the original Committee all resigned, one by one, and this underlying staff problem resolved itself in a most unusual way.

Under some pressure from Lambeth Council, which had long complained about conditions at the Marmite shelter and its many contraventions of the local planning and health regulations, the GLC had been trying to find St Mungo alternative accommodation. Initially, it was suggested that St Mungo might move to Tress House in Stamford Street, Southwark, a large and somewhat dilapidated office building that was standing empty and was expected to remain unoccupied for a further three or four years pending redevelopment of the area. However, Southwark Borough Council emphasised that however much they might sympathise with the problems of the homeless they did not want too many in Stamford Street. The GLC then offered another building, a former warehouse at 55 Bondway, that was close to Lennox Buildings, and near the approach road to Vauxhall Bridge in Lambeth.

Arrangements for St Mungo to acquire the Bondway building were discussed throughout the period of the Section 19 investigation by the Housing Corporation, the charging of Jim Horne and the reconstitution of the board of the St Mungo Community Housing Association Ltd, but given all these circumstances neither the GLC nor the Housing Corporation felt able to recommend a formal agreement with St Mungo until all these matters had been resolved. Eventually it was agreed that UHAT (the United Housing Associations Trust Ltd) should manage the conversion of 55 Bondway on St Mungo's behalf.

The Bondway night shelter became the first major single homeless project to be jointly agreed by the Housing Corporation, the GLC and the Department of the Environment. The conversion costs totalled approximately £200,000, and this was funded on the basis that Bondway would be able to provide basic shelter each night for 125 homeless men for at least thirty years. The go-ahead for the project was given on condition that St Mungo agreed to vacate the Marmite factory, and while UHAT was in charge of the conversion of the warehouse premises the Marmite project closed and its staff were seconded to UHAT on a temporary basis. However, once the Project Leader, Graham Parr, and his staff were in occupation at Bondway they made it plain that they did not want St Mungo back. The atmosphere became highly charged because it was Mr Parr who had laid the information with the Housing Corporation that led to the criminal charges against Jim Horne. Tempers ran high. The local Member of Parliament, Stuart Holland, supported Graham Parr and the staff – and so did Antony Fletcher, who served on the board of the Housing Corporation, and took up the staff's case with the Corporation Chairman, Hugh Cubitt.

In the end, after many meetings and much acrimony, St Mungo pulled out of the Bondway project and its former staff ended up helping to form the Bondway Housing Association Ltd, with the continuing support of Mr Holland and others. In all fairness, it has to be acknowledged that Bondway has made an important contribution to London homelessness, providing food and

shelter each night for the desperately homeless, with
back-up facilities such as medical care and chiropody
services which are an essential part of this work. Its birth
may have been an untidy affair, but, as may have been
noticed already in this narrative, there was nothing particularly neat or orthodox about the whole of this endeav-
our to help London's single homeless.[6]

By now the St Mungo Community Housing Association
had a new Director, John Lane, and there were some who
feared that he might have to oversee its demise. St
Mungo seemed to be suffering death by a thousand cuts.
With the new owners of the Charing Cross Hospital
building, the Metropolitan Police, now pressing for
possession, and Bondway slipping away from its hands,
St Mungo seemed to have some strange sword of Damo-
cles hanging over it. The whole project seemed doomed.

---

[6] While going through his very thick files on the Bondway project and the
internecine disputes relating thereto, the author found one memo from
the then GLC Controller of Housing, Harry Simpson, containing the
advice that this was a difficult issue that needed consideration 'on levels
other than theoretical correctness'. This was good advice that reflected
the spirit of the time.

Chapter 7

Before coming to St Mungo's, John Lane was a restless clergyman looking for a true vocation. On leaving Burnley Grammar School at the age of 16, he had spent three years training to be a quantity surveyor but found the work 'a bit turgid'. He then spent four years studying at the Methodist theological college at Handsworth, Birmingham, before taking up his first post in South Wales. After two years as a minister at Llanharan, near Cardiff, he returned to Lancashire, spending three years at Great Harwood, near Blackburn. There he acquired his first experience of voluntary work.

Great Harwood is a small industrial town with a population of 8,000. His arrival in 1964 coincided with the appointment of new parsons by both the local Anglicans and the Congregationalists.

> The three of us took the town by storm. The local rag thought it was marvellous. All they had to do was see us every Monday morning, and they could fill the paper for the week. Between us, we reorganised the local youth clubs on a town basis instead of a church basis, and also set up a club for the disabled ... and then I became a representative on the Lancashire Education Committee, and became involved with the local Labour Party. That gave me my first understanding that one could move on from the traditional ministerial role to become meaningful and useful outside the Church.

From there, Lane moved to London, spending five years as a minister in Lewisham before turning to full-time voluntary work with his appointment as Director of the Peckham Settlement, in 1972. Elspeth Howe, wife of the present Foreign Secretary, was the President, taking a busy interest in the everyday life of the settlement. The Chairman was the former England cricket captain David

Sheppard, then Bishop of Woolwich and now Bishop of Liverpool.

'My move to Peckham was a very deliberate step out of parish work into the voluntary sector,' says Lane, 'I had started to have doubts about the Free Church while I was still at College, beginning to believe that life is not about cerebral things but aesthetics ... the Free Church is much more cerebral, concerned with ideas and words, whereas now I find I've become a fairly High Church Anglican, almost Roman Catholic, concerned more with people and wonder than ideas.'

Lane spent six years at Peckham. When he arrived there was a staff of two. By the time he left there were twenty full-time staff and a small army of volunteers.

When I went there it was still a very traditional settlement. It had a nursery school, a playgroup and lots of old people's clubs. We branched out into community work, establishing residents' associations, an adventure playground, a very large West Indian community organisation (which we then backed out of, leaving them to run it themselves), youth work, particularly with black kids, including a residential home and a work creation project. We also developed what was known as the Urban Study Centre. The settlement had been founded by girls' public schools, and we were supported by schools like Wycombe Abbey, Roedean and Benenden. The tradition was that they came down to Peckham to do good, dressed in their boaters, but we turned the process round and said, 'You can come to Peckham so long as you don't wear your boaters, and as long as you realise that you are not coming to "do good" for Peckham. You're coming to learn what life is like.'

I'm a great believer in settlements. Elspeth Howe threw herself into it all, and so it was quite interesting because the Shadow Chancellor's wife (as she was then) was involved in community work in Peckham, and on the board she and the Bishop were meeting black community leaders. It was a very healthy mix.

From there, Lane moved to the national office of the Young Women's Christian Association as part public relations officer, part fund raiser. Realising that he had made a mistake ('I hated the job'), he found himself scouring the Jobs Vacant sections of the newspapers and it was through an advertisement in *The Guardian* that he heard of St Mungo's. 'Apparently, it had been advertised before in *The Daily Telegraph*. They didn't get anyone suitable, and in the state they were in at the time, moving from one regime to another, with the Housing Corporation appointees running the Board, they thought they ought to get the kind of applicant who would read that section of *The Telegraph*. Instead, they got me.'

By the time Lane took up the appointment, St Mungo's had been without a Director for approximately twelve months. Technically, Jim Horne was still the Director. His appointment was in suspense pending the outcome of the court proceedings (a situation that was almost bound to cause tensions between the two of them, and did). In the meantime, St Mungo's had been run by a few active members of the Board, rotating the chairmanship between them. Charing Cross, by far the largest part of the whole operation, had been managed almost single-handedly by a Glaswegian, Tom Campbell, who had a natural empathy with the residents. A former professional boxer and one-time footballer for Glasgow Celtic, Campbell had been in gaol himself. Like many of the people who worked for St Mungo, he had a criminal record. 'He worshipped Jim Horne,' says Lane, who recognises that there was at that period a quite definite criminal subculture within St Mungo's (or, it might be said, St Mungo's itself formed part of central London's criminal under class). To a certain extent, this will always be so, and St Mungo's could not be effective unless it was.

'There is a certain kind of honesty between men who have been in prison, the Army, the Navy or the lump-labour sector of society,' Lane noticed, 'and they respond

John Lane

well when they are managed by one of their own ... in his own way, Tom Campbell was quite brilliant. He was marvellous with the residents, organising football teams, day outings to France and Belgium, and mass bookings to see Billy Connolly.' He was on their wavelength. When the resettlement team came in to help rehouse them they would laboriously come up with solutions which he reached instinctively.

Lane also appreciates that in that intervening period, when the Housing Corporation, the DHSS, the Department of the Environment and the GLC were all looking rather anxiously at the problems posed by Charing Cross, the Board seized control of the Association. It would be difficult now to say who did what. Some members of the Board were hardly seen. Others, like Francis Bergin and Bob Greenshields, took on the responsibility for senior staff appointments and finance. The Housing Corporation appointees, Mrs Joan Forsyth and Tony Shephard, were meticulous in their requirements (which was the reason why they were there).

Internally, there was also a body called the Interim Management Group which comprised Ron Upton, the Warden at Hammersmith, and Sarah Matheson plus four outside consultants, Ian Zass-Ogilvie (UHAT), the auditors Richard Jackson and Richard Marke, and Derek Joseph from Housing Associations Consultancy and Advisory Service. It was this group that really made the running, meeting regularly, and then making recommendations to the Board. They sorted out all the things like pay scales, conditions of employment, contracts of employment, and budgetary requirements.

I am sure that between me going in and Jim leaving, they had done a good job, pulling the whole thing together. There was a lot of sweat, a lot of dreadful administrative detail to sort out, horrendous ... I could not have done that myself. They sorted out a rigmarole, and put St Mungo's on the path of establishing an organisation, although I would maintain that until Tom Campbell went no one had control over the Association. He was the great archetypal figure during that period when Jim Horne was building up Charing Cross, and then afterwards when Jim had been charged by the police.

Tom was a bluff Glaswegian. He knew his boxing and his football, and had been a professional gambler. He was very macho, separated from his wife, with two sons, both of whom got into serious trouble with the police . . . Tom felt very bad about them. Tom was incredibly soft, and when he had been drinking he used to cry about the way he had treated his family, but he had that great macho Glaswegian exterior. That was what he presented, but he wouldn't get rid of bad staff and he wouldn't get rid of violent residents. I can't think, offhand, of one member of staff that he sacked, or one resident that he threw out. Doubtless, there were some, but that wasn't his style.

In his first weeks at St Mungo's, John Lane faced crises of every kind. At his first meeting with Graham Parr, who was responsible for the transitional management at Bondway, he was harangued for two and a half hours. 'Graham felt that he hadn't been told what was going on, and was deeply aggrieved, I think with some justi-fication,' says Lane. Within Charing Cross, staff and residents all felt embattled. There was loyalty to Jim Horne, who had built the whole thing up, and a deep-held feeling that he had been unjustly accused. Horne was expected to return (not least by Horne himself, who kept in touch with both residents and staff). Equally, in the wake of *Goodbye Longfellow Road* and all the other dramas there was a strong determination on the part of the funding authorities that there should be no more scandals. All expenditure was now rigorously monitored, and Lane was left in little doubt that he was himself on probation. At the time he seemed quite bemused by it all.

Bondway was his first real test. The project had been funded by the GLC with the express purpose of helping St Mungo's become a more conventional charity, operating from better premises and with trained staff. No one wanted any more Marmite shelters.

I had that meeting with Graham Parr, and remember him, together with the chairman of his committee, Linda Vellacot, literally shouting at me for two and a half hours about the ways in which St Mungo had failed the staff and how I was not equipped to be the Director. He was slamming this file up and down on the table. He claimed, rightly so, that he had had far more experience in the field of single homeless than probably anybody on the committee and had done a great deal of painstaking work. I decided more or less straight away that it was impossible for St Mungo to take Bondway in, but that I couldn't say this to the Committee because I hadn't had time to prove myself to them. So I insisted that certain members of the Committee went along to Bondway, and it was they who would have to persuade me not to take Bondway over. We saw a vision of television cameras watching bailiffs going in and throwing the staff out because they would undoubtedly have occupied the place. That would have been bad publicity just when we were trying to find resources to replace Charing Cross.

I think it was the right decision in the end. Frankly, thank God we haven't got Bondway, anyway. It would have been fine as part of a chain of accommodation like we've got now, but had we had it at the beginning we probably wouldn't have developed the same chain. It's become one step up from the soup kitchen and it's very poor semi-permanent accommodation. People have been there for three or four years. It has partitions between the beds about 4 feet high. They empty the place every day and hose it down and it is not in any sense a home.

Lane also had to deal with the equally difficult problem of Lennox Buildings, the complex of run-down, semi-derelict flats, close to Bondway. The site was needed for a highways scheme, and he was required to clear the premises. By then, there were eighty men living there, many of whom had previously been in mental hospitals or prison, or both.

There was a lot of violence and massive thieving of rent, and I later discovered that in one three-month period only fifty pence had been collected from *all* the electric meters. We had one very nasty fire there when a resident brought back one of his mates from the pub at closing-time. The resident fell fast asleep on the bed, drunk, and his mate fell asleep in a chair, and one them dropped a lighted cigarette which set fire to the furniture. It was that nasty foam furniture, and there was a tremendous fire in which the resident was killed ... the buildings were in an appalling state, but some of the men refused to leave and we had to get court orders against them and then bring the bailiffs in. And then one morning the GLC came in and bulldozed down the whole complex.

Facing these different crises, Lane had three strong cards to play. The Housing Corporation had told him they would fund replacement units for Charing Cross where the police now wanted vacant possession to redevelop the site. He had been promised assistance from government departments, the GLC and the central London boroughs to ensure that no one was made homeless by the Charing Cross closure, and he knew that the last thing they all wanted was to have to find a new Director and start all over again.

Finding replacements for Charing Cross proved a nightmare. Lane circularised 8,000 estate agents, and then followed them up twice. His staff also walked the London streets looking for empty buildings that might be suitable for conversion. The Metropolitan Police Commissioner even made the police launch available so that they could travel up and down the river Thames seeing what other buildings might not be visible from land. 'We tried everything we could think of. We got publicity in the Press, on the radio, on television, and it took us over a year before we found our first building in Lancaster Road. That's a building with ten beds which came to us from a housing association.'

Their first major break-through came with the hostel

at Cromwell Road which they bought from a small hotel chain. It had been a nurses' home and was called Nightingale House. St Mungo's bought the building freehold for £550,000, with a mortgage from the Housing Corporation and top-up funding from the Home Office and the GLC. Accommodation is provided there for eighty men, mostly in separate rooms. There are eighteen staff.

His next coup, which happened around the same time (the one was found first and the other opened first), was the new St Mungo hostel in Endell Street, just off Shaftesbury Avenue in Covent Garden. The building had originally been a parish school, with rooms on five floors, and then became a YMCA for several years. The YMCA left it when they opened a new purpose-built hostel in Great Russell Street, and then it was squatted. The first time St Mungo tried to buy the building, they were outbid by a firm of property developers, who modernised the building as a new hostel for Bedford College. 'In the end, Bedford didn't want it and we picked it up very cheap – for £1,030,000' says Lane, who reckons the site alone is now worth £10m. The hostel now provides accommodation for 110 residents. There is a staff of twenty-five.

Endell Street and Cromwell Road lie at the heart of St Mungo's present work for the homeless. The Association is now organised with two regional managers, Brian Boylan (Eastern Region) and Charles Fraser (Western Region), who both started initially at Charing Cross. They are responsible for the day-to-day administration of projects within their areas.

Eastern Region

This region is grouped around Endell Street, which provides accommodation for men in central London who come in, literally, off the streets. The staff there liaise with London soup runs and advice agencies to provide this service, keeping the hostel open twenty-four hours a day with supervisors on duty during eight-hour shifts. Statistics show that 30 per cent of all new arrivals at Endell Street suffer from some form of mental illness; 15 per cent have alcohol dependency problems, and another 15 per cent are either elderly or infirm. Less than a third of those arriving at Endell Street are people who are simply homeless, with no other significant emotional or personal problems. All new residents are interviewed by resettlement staff with a view to helping them move on to other St Mungo projects or independent accommodation. Those who need it are also encouraged to go on training courses, to learn how to cook and handle everyday problems, as part of their preparation for being found a home of their own.

An essential part of this process is the use of the other St Mungo projects within the region so that there is a fairly constant throughput, enabling the staff to move people on from Endell Street and keep beds available for new arrivals. The other projects in the region are at *Tufnell Park Road, London N7* (twelve beds for elderly or infirm men who have a drink problem); *Huddleston Road, London N7* (seven beds for men who must be able to cook and look after themselves, thus preparing them for a place of their own); *Brecknock Road, London N19* (nine beds with a similar policy to Huddleston Road, with the emphasis on independent living; those who are out of work are also encouraged to take part in an employment training programme); *Argyle Street, London WC1* (eighteen beds for homeless men, many of them mentally ill, needing a high level of support, although they are encouraged to cook and look after themselves); *Wharton Street, London WC1* (the first St Mungo hostel to be opened specially for women, providing eleven beds); a scheme for five houses in *Rosebery Avenue, London N1*, next door to the Sadlers Wells Theatre (these had been empty for fifteen years and have been converted into a cluster of flats and bed-sits for twenty-nine people, both men and women), and a pioneering scheme in *Court Gardens, Islington,* where six Portakabins have been erected on a landscaped site to provide self-contained units for people who were formerly in bed-and-breakfast accommodation (at half the cost).

Western Region

This region is grouped around the Cromwell Road hostel, which is also staffed on a twenty-four hours a day basis. Often the homeless people who arrive here are younger than at Endell Street, and there is thus a wide-ranging advisory service providing help on rehousing, employment, medical, financial and other more personal problems, such as drugs or alcohol dependency. Cromwell Road has eighty beds, and from here residents can be moved on to another thirty-bed hostel at *Adamson Road, London NW3* and smaller projects at *Bravington Road, London W9* (nine beds with shared kitchen and living room); two schemes in *Lancaster Road, London W11*(both with eight beds, with two bedrooms and a kitchen on each floor); two schemes in *Shirland Road, London W9* (one with six beds and the other with twelve, again with fully fitted kitchens and shared sitting rooms); *Chippenham Road, London W9* (a shared house with six beds, a kitchen and sitting room); *Oakley Square, London N1* (a shared short-life hostel with seven beds, two kitchens and a sitting room); *Claremont Road, London W9* (a group home with six beds, shared sitting room, dining room and kitchen), and *Charlton Kings Road, London NW5* (a group home with four beds, a shared sitting room, dining room and kitchen).

In addition to all these projects, which have been mostly acquired and refurbished over the past five years, St

Mungo's also has others in its development programme. These include a three-storey office building at *217 Harrow Road, London W2*, which had previously been used as a psychotherapy centre. The building was acquired from the GLC three years ago, and has recently been adapted to provide a high-care hostel for thirty residents; premises for a retraining project, and central offices for the Association on the top floor.

Also in the present development programme is a scheme in *Albion Grove, Hackney* (a 29-bed hostel); *Mornington Terrace, London N1* (another shared house for eight people), and the former *Camden Road Baptist Church, London* (now being converted into a hostel for thirty-four people with a club house, and other educational and recreational facilities).

By the time this present programme is completed, St Mungo will have over 500 beds available every night, so enabling it to take a constant flow of homeless people off the streets of London, through its direct access hostels into these more self-contained units where they can either learn or re-establish the habit of looking after themselves, as a preparation for moving into their own accommodation. Through this process, over 400 homeless men have already found homes of their own, although there are others who may have to stay longer in the different St Mungo projects; some for the rest of their lives, because their problems are such that they need the support that St Mungo's trained welfare staff are able to give them.

Chapter 8

Central to the whole story of St Mungo's is what happened at Charing Cross. For nine years, until its closure on 5 May 1983, this complex right at the heart of London, just off Trafalgar Square, was widely seen as a running social sore, although some of St Mungo's longer-serving staff would argue that it achieved much in providing a haven for the destitute. The building itself was sliding into dereliction. Destitute men hung around its entrance in Agar Street, hair dank, clothes dirty, often clasping quart bottles of cider and stout. The whole area stank. Police were constantly running in and out of the building – literally, running – chasing thieves and shoplifters.

No one ever knew how many men were sleeping there, but it is now realised that many nights there were more than the declared 550, and nearly four times the numbers stipulated by the GLC. Some nights, particularly Thursdays (which was the day the men's GIRO money came through), there would be widespread drunkenness in the area. The staff tried to prevent fighting but it did happen; one resident died of injuries received in a drunken brawl. Hygiene was a constant problem. Cats roamed the building, at least keeping the mice under control. Bed linen was sometimes so filthy that the laundry would not handle it, and the condition of one room became so bad that the staff removed the residents and boarded it up. Prostitutes sometimes worked their way through the dormitories when it was known that money was flowing freely. This was almost impossible to control because, although the main entrance was manned twenty-four hours a day, the building had been a hospital and there were six other unmanned entrances through which medical supplies and fuel had originally been taken into the premises when it was built as a hospital. Homeless men already inside Charing Cross were forever opening these doors to let more people in, sometimes so that they could charge them 'rent' for the night.

Because of its past use, the building itself was a warren of corridors and dormitories, some accommodating thirty or forty men in long lines of beds along each wall, while those who had graduated from this part of the St Mungo's operation were housed in single rooms in the adjoining building, the former nurses' home which had a separate entrance from Chandos Street.

Three of John Lane's senior colleagues, Mick Carroll, Charles Fraser and Brian Boylan, came to Charing Cross in 1980. Carroll, now Manager at Endell Street, arrived in the August. Fraser, now Western Regional Manager, came in the October, as did Brian Boylan, now Eastern Regional Manager, a Catholic priest who had previously worked in a squatter district in Manila and another remote rural area of the Philippines. All three men helped with the transition from Charing Cross to the present. This chapter is partly based on their recollections; on those of other St Mungo staff and residents, and press reports.

The first thing that any visitor noticed when arriving at Charing Cross was the smell. This wasn't the usual hostel smell of old socks, but, as one member of staff described it, 'a mixture of cat's piss, shit and a general decomposition of every kind of material in the building, mixed with rotting rubbish, and the marsh gas rising from the basement'. Down below the cellars and the boiler rooms there was a whole complex of underground tunnels that were permanently under water. These had been dug out during the First World War when the Government thought it would not have been good for civilian morale for people to see so many wounded soldiers returning from France. Apparently, trains carrying the wounded were arriving regularly at Charing Cross station from the ports on the Kent coast. The wounded were then taken through these tunnels into the hospital. Other tunnels led to nearby buildings which had been temporarily taken over, including St Peter's Hospital in Henrietta Street. Corpses were taken through another tunnel to the School of Tropical Hygiene where doctors were studying the effects of mustard gas.

Keeping these buildings adequately heated was a problem throughout St Mungo's occupation. This was 'assisted' by one of the residents, Steve, a drug casualty from the sixties, whose brain had been damaged by constant use of LSD. Periodically, Steve would go berserk, and then this normally quiet little man, who was said to look a little like Catweasel, became so violent that a dozen policemen always had to be sent to hold him down and then take him off to a mental hospital. At other times, Steve would sit in the boiler room, talking to the boilers, and if they did not say the right things to him he would take a spanner to them.

On the ground floor, directly above the boilers, St Mungo had set aside a room for the older residents. Shortly before Charing Cross closed there was nearly a disaster when Steve jammed the emergency valve of the boiler system open with a block of wood while he was spaced-out during one of his encounters with the boilers. This was a cut-out valve and he believed that the boiler was prone to react to excess pressure by releasing the steam and shutting itself down, which meant there wasn't enough heat coming through to the residents' room upstairs – and so in order to ensure their warmth he overruled the safety mechanism with this block of wood. A passer-by saw smoke billowing out of the top of the chimney stack and called the fire brigade, who arrived in force to find that the casing of the boiler had all but melted through with the build-up of heat and pressure inside the furnace. They were horrified, and told the staff that within an hour there would have been an enormous explosion that might have sent the whole building skywards.

Another resident thought he would help St Mungo's finances by wiring the electricity supply up to that of the Civil Service Stores, and managed to get the wiring within one foot of their supply point before he was detected.

The lasting memory that staff and residents have of the building was of the general feeling of dereliction. Doors hanging off hinges. Loos, baths and washbasins usually broken, and pipes leaking, with perished plaster everywhere. Near the main entrance there was a 'shop', a room where soup and food were provided, which was a good 'casual' for the men who could pick up fifteen quid for working there in the evenings. When the electric kettle was plugged into the mains (it was a large catering kettle with a broken handle), cockroaches would crawl out of the spout. That summed up the physical state of the building. The place was a slum and yet it was full nearly every night, usually with 550 men sleeping there, and sometimes more. Camp beds were folded away in unused rooms, and these would be rolled down to cater for extra numbers.

When the staff came to clear the building out in 1983, they found beds hidden away in different parts of the building where people had been living without them knowing they were there. There were people living in cupboards, and one bed was even found behind a false ceiling. This was all part of the black economy that existed within the complex; some of these nooks and crannies and concealed cubbyholes were rented out by the residents, to supplement their GIRO money. 'There was a lot of subletting,' says John Lane, 'and I don't think any of the supervisors realised the scale of it until the building was empty.' It was a constant problem for the people who were supposedly supervising activities there. Because it had been a hospital, and there were all these different points of access, the staff couldn't possibly be aware of all that was going on. Theoretically, security was watertight – but there was access through the boiler rooms, through the kitchen area, through the waste disposal, and through the entrances where all the hospital deliveries had come into the building, and a walkway all round the building linking all these different access points. People were always coming in and out, and fiddling the system in their own little ways, and this contributed to some of the atmosphere that was there. Everyone mucked in together.

This slightly chaotic, if not anarchic, situation appealed to many of the residents. Many of them had been in the Forces, in prison or in hospital, and were used to living in an all-male environment. They tended to identify with the Manager, Tom Campbell, a tough Glaswegian, who was keenly interested in boxing, football and betting.

Campbell would walk around the building with a large wad of notes in his back pocket, and whenever there were bills to be paid he would peel off the notes and pay them in cash, pocketing the receipt. In his office there was a large cupboard in which he kept all his money. Once a week he would settle up, and send the balance upstairs. Sometimes, his takings and his winnings would all end up in the same cupboard. Every bill was always settled, but Tom was never a conventional administrator. However, he did generate a lot of respect among the residents who shared his interests and, often, his background, and there were times when Campbell would appear to be defending them against other members of the staff. At staff meetings, Lane would make a proposal and then say, 'What do you think, Tom?' and the staff would sit there in silence, knowing that this might be an incursion upon his territory, and waiting for him to say, as he often would, 'I don't think *that* would be in the interests of the residents.' The men, however, were very affectionate towards him, and he, in turn, thought the world of Jim Horne.

Although there is now a very different pattern of management throughout St Mungo's, the present staff recognise that both Campbell and Horne had that rare knack of handling large numbers of difficult men. While Campbell was in charge, he was regularly running an establishment that accommodated as many as 550 men a night, taking them off the streets and giving them shelter, and providing them with good basic food. There were three dining rooms, and Campbell was determined that every resident should have food of a nutritious quality. Every morning when they came down there was a cooked breakfast with porridge followed by a choice of egg, bacon, sausage, beans or tomato, toast and a cup of tea. The breakfast was included in the charge for the night's accommodation, and then if the residents wanted it there was also an evening meal, which they paid for separately. The staff used to drive down to Smithfield Market at 5.30 in the morning to get the week's meat, always buying meat of the best quality at competitive prices. On Fridays there would be fish from Billingsgate. Throughout the week, there would be good quality vegetables, always bought cheaply and in quantity in the markets. Campbell was very economical in ways like this.

Christmas was always a great occasion. On Campbell's instructions, there was a special Christmas breakfast, and then later in the day, the Christmas Dinner, with roast turkey, plum pudding, and all the trimmings. Then out of the Welfare Fund that he had established, presents would be provided for all the residents – packets of cigarettes, small items of clothing like socks or underpants, or toothpaste and brush, which all meant a lot to the men (it's important to remember that homeless men often need the day-to-day essentials that most of us take for granted).

Another quality that the residents liked in Campbell was that if there was anything that they wanted, better food, a different bed, or whatever, they could go to him and get an answer. Unlike the DHSS or the other authorities that they were used to dealing with, Campbell would always say 'Yes' or 'No', and deal with it. The men received an immediate response, and many of them found that very reassuring.

Campbell's authority was underlined by the fact that he was a Glaswegian and many of the residents, and staff, also came from Scotland. The hard-drinking Scots labourers, drawn to London by the lure of high wages, felt at home there, whereas a young West Indian would not have done; this became self-perpetuating because these Scots were sometimes men for whom 'a wee jar' meant eighteen pints at lunch-time.

One newcomer noted that this was then a large part of St Mungo's clientele,

the dour, drinking labouring classes; itinerant mobile labourers, and others who had been and were now broken down in health, either mentally or physically ... when I went there the atmosphere was like a Wild West town. There were people working as demolition gangs who booked in en masse from Doncaster, or whatever. When they were in London earning £600 a week, you would get these huge brawls breaking out late at night after they had come back from the West End pubs and clubs. They were earning fistfuls of money and all we were charging then (this was 1980) was about seven quid a week for bed and breakfast, and then they paid extra for an evening meal on top of that ... and then it went up to twelve quid, and then £17.50, at which point the gangs started moving out.

These guys were coming back from the demolition sites in the early evenings in their boots and jeans, and then they would go upstairs, have a wash in one of those cracked basins, splash Old Spice all over themselves, and go off to the West End. On their way back they would break into the cigarette machines in the area, and the police would follow them home. There was a lot of petty crime, and they were able to get their hands on enough money to be able to get very drunk nearly every day.

Some of the men used to go shoplifting, more or less to

order. The place was full of Parker pens, Ronson lighters and electric clocks. There was also a constant supply of fresh salmon and bottles of Scotch. One day a guy came back there with three dozen Charles and Di wedding plates . . . he and others used to descend upon a local department store, and if the manager there thought it was a good idea to put out a gondola full of Charles and Di wedding gear, this guy would be watching, knowing exactly where they were screwing up their security, and then he would be in there, loading up his bag and out of the back door.

Tom Campbell presided over all this with good humour and kindness, defending the residents, sometimes even turning up in court for them when they needed a reference, commanding widespread respect because he was regarded by them as 'one of the boys'. This is illustrated by an anecdote concerning a resident named Tom Dillon (whom we shall meet in the next chapter). Dillon was behind with his rent, and for some weeks he had been slipping in and out of the building, avoiding Campbell with care. One day he misjudged his timing, and had come too close to the main entrance before realising that Campbell was standing there at the desk, and so Dillon averted his eyes and tried to slip past unnoticed.

'Aboot your rent, Mr Dillon,' said Campbell, in his broad Glaswegian accent.

Dillon stopped, looked anxiously from side to side, assessing his moments to safety, and said in his own equally distinctive Irish accent, 'They were running neck and neck to the final fence, and your rent went down . . .'

Each morning Campbell would walk around the building, checking the dormitories, chasing unpaid rents (about which he was strict), taking an interest in all the residents' minor woes. 'He exuded care for the individual,' says Boylan, recalling one incident that demonstrates the feeling that was developed at Charing Cross (and which St Mungo's has not lost, for all the changes that have occurred in recent years).

There was one man who was dying and was in considerable discomfort. On three separate occasions I called for an ambulance, but each time he refused to go to hospital and pleaded with me to be left in his own bed. For him, this was home, and he had such a genteel, very English manner, with the refined accent that comes from middle-class upbringing, that I realised that he had known other ways of living . . . but for him, facing death, this was home and he did not want to leave. We allowed him to stay until he went into a coma. For me, that typifies the way the men felt about the community that we established at Charing Cross. In every possible sense, it was a community and we all know we owed a lot to Tom Campbell . . . here were all these outcasts, alcoholics and winos, living together, and *paying rent* . . . this wasn't a Church-based concept, offering salvation. These men were living in a community, *paying rent*, which gave them the right to complain about the food, or to ask for a better bed. The care that was provided was never patronising. It was neither seductive, nor exploitive nor manipulative, and that ethos developed still further when John Lane arrived here. We totally debunked the Salvation-idea. We weren't trying to save anyone. We were providing a service for which the men paid *rent*, and that became the basis of our contract; of the relationship between the men and the staff.

This was the positive side of the Charing Cross experiment. It was never easy. Homeless men reduced to these conditions do pose unusual problems. On one occasion, two men died in a fire that broke out shortly after the whole establishment had been put through a fire drill by the staff. The men had clearly ignored the safety instructions. 'I was able to live with those consequences without any feelings of guilt, and I put that down to the management ethos that John Lane has created here,' says Boylan.

Lane himself says that the most difficult single decision that he had to take during his early period at St Mungo's was resolving that he would have to remove Campbell, 'because he was so close to the residents, in thinking and in outlook, that I believed that we couldn't progress while he was still running the show ... we couldn't change the nature of the relationship between the residents and the staff while Tom was still there'.

Lane's difficulty lay in his realisation that Campbell was popular with residents and many staff. He was tough and jovial; a man's man, who was at his happiest organising outings for the men, drinking with them, and debating the fortunes of Glasgow Celtic or the latest Scottish boxer to be challenging for a title. However, Lane believed it was this very geniality that made it difficult for St Mungo's to progress; he considered that St Mungo's had to acquire a different style of management, and then through this become a more stable community. This is a difficult dilemma to describe because the problems themselves were not of Campbell's causing; he was running an establishment that catered for men who could be very difficult. What was at issue was how St Mungo's tried to help them – by identifying with their problems in the Campbell way, or offering them something different.

One staff member who worked there through that period told me:

> Tom was always a great strength to the residents, because he facilitated them running around in a mess, which was what a lot of them wanted to do. That's why they liked him. They were like 5-year-olds, playing around in the mud, and the consequences of their actions were entirely divorced from their experience ... it was not uncommon for police to chase residents into the building, and for the residents then to disappear. Charing Cross became a bolthole where everyone was welcome, thick as thieves, and all that kind of thing. The police would run in and be confronted by a maze and blank looks from the staff ... sometimes, late at night, there was violence. I went there one night and saw a member of the staff being held by a Scotsman with a broken bottle there (neck) and a knife down there (ribs), while this member of staff was gently talking him down. This was a fairly extreme example, but violence did happen fairly regularly at nights.

Whenever staff tried to deal with violence, they would be met by blank stares. Late at night a man might totter down the main corridor, with blood streaming from a head wound, and when asked what had happened would invariably say, 'Dunno. Walked into a door.' The residents would never split on each other, a lesson that they had learned through being in other all-male environments, like the Army or prison. They were all thoroughly bonded, because that was their code. The one thing no man ever does in prison is 'grass' – and it was the same in Charing Cross.

And yet, once Lane had taken his decision and Campbell had been given notice, his support among the residents seemed to evaporate. There was some difficulty over his final leaving, because he had been living in a flat at Charing Cross and was given notice, and the day before he left he had gone round the building, telling his old cronies that he would be moving tomorrow and would appreciate some help – and not one man went to help him carry his furniture.

With Campbell's departure and the dispersal of the residents from Charing Cross, with approximately fifty of them moving with the staff to Endell Street; some to other hostels, or (where they were capable of it) into their own accommodation, this extraordinary era came to an end. St Mungo's had been in Charing Cross for exactly nine years, from May 1974 until May 1983. Many thousands of homeless men had passed through, and it was perhaps a typical epitaph on the whole enterprise that shortly before the final departure the police raided the premises yet again, having discovered that a team of residents were now stripping lead from the roof.

There was one room that had hardly ever been used, and when the police went inside they found two tons of lead neatly stacked on the floor, waiting to be shipped out. Nobody knows how much other lead had already gone because the whole place was covered in lead. Apart from the roof, there were miles of lead piping and even the window-sills were all made of lead, and, of course, the men realised that this was money, but they didn't stop to think (as they never did) that the police now owned the building, and the one thing you don't do is steal from the police! One man got two years for that, and several others were also dealt with by the courts.

Now, with the dispersal of the old regime and the death of many of the older residents who moved to Endell Street, St Mungo's is gradually changing – without losing its street credibility. Apart from one small hostel for women opened in 1987, and the development at Rosebery Avenue, Islington, which caters for both men and women, St Mungo's is still largely an all-male establishment, with a broader intake these days (not so many Scots and a wider age range), and yet still retaining much of that prison, Army or Navy ethos that seems to be an indelible characteristic of the work it does.

'Some of the staff form attachments to the kind of characters that are drawn to St Mungo's,' says Mick Carroll.

There's real affection for the man who always *must* be directing traffic outside Endell Street, because all he needs is a sniff of the barmaid's apron and he's completely loopy … particularly, as often happens, when they combine that kind of behaviour with enormous intelligence and personalities which, had they not had a major head injury or had something go terribly wrong with their lives, would have enabled them to live very differently. It's surprising how many of the men have had industrial accidents, or reached the end of labouring lives with no means to provide for themselves, and have yet acquired vast knowledge. We have had people here who have travelled all over the world, but been brain damaged when they have gone on a building site without a protective hat. A lot of the people who are with us now were lump labour in the fifties, came over from Ireland or down from Glasgow, lived eight to a room, handled large sums of cash – and now have nothing to show for it. If they got injured on a site, they were the ones that turned up at Charing Cross and seemed to haunt the place all the time I was there.

Inevitably, there are risks in running an enterprise like St Mungo's. This sector that Paddy O'Connor and Jim Horne set out to help in opening the doors at Charing Cross is always there within society. Those people mentioned in the first chapter, who confront you if you miss that late night train, still walk the city streets looking for refuge in places like St Mungo's, sometimes rejecting what they have to offer because their lives have slipped too far, sometimes so troubled by mental illness that even St Mungo's cannot help them.

Within St Mungo's now there are two men with great natural skills as painters who could undoubtedly have had careers as artists but for schizophrenia and dependence on alcohol, and there are others whom the staff *know* may at any time suffer some form of brainstorm. (Since the move to Endell Street, there has been one tragic incident when a resident climbed into the aperture above the lift shaft, doused himself with oil and then set fire to himself; he took twenty minutes to die – and kept the fire brigade at bay by claiming to have a bomb. Damage was so extensive that repairs to the roof area cost £200,000.)

And yet someone has to love them . . .

Chapter 9

To really understand what St Mungo's is all about, and what Paddy O'Connor, Jim Horne, John Lane and its present staff have all been trying to achieve, you have to meet the homeless. Apart from a certain frailty, they are much like the rest of us: People. There is little point relying upon surveys on them and why they are homeless because these are always deceiving. Whether conducted second-hand through compiling figures kept by advice agencies, or face to face by interviewers ticking off squares on a clipboard, all they represent are numbers and categories. Numerals on a printed page can never tell the whole story, for what we are talking about is: People. Every single homeless person on the streets of London, wandering through station subways, lying in a doorway, queuing for food or begging for money, has a different story to tell. Each individual human being has lived a separate life, and it is only the common fact of being *homeless* that brings them together at all.

Many are former soldiers or seamen, or unmarried men of working-class origin, reflecting the fact that much of our society's manual work is done by unskilled men, often Scottish or Irish, who are paid in cash as casual labourers or employed so occasionally that they never earn enough to marry or acquire a home of their own. Many are single, but it would be wrong to categorise them too neatly for each has a story to tell. Here are the stories of eight of them. None is typical (because there is no such being as a 'typical' homeless person). They have all been homeless and came to St Mungo because they had nowhere else to live. In a curious way, some have remained a part of the Community long after they have left.

*Looking out of the window of a bus or driving down St
Martin's Lane, you may have seen Harry Scroggie. Most
days, rain or shine – at 12.00 noon and 3.00 pm – he
stands out there by the railings, just opposite the Shaftesbury Theatre, where traffic turns down to Piccadilly
Circus. Harry Scroggie is the man with his hand out-
stretched. All the pigeons know him, so does the blackbird
that sings in a backyard bush off Covent Garden, the
sparrows that live in the downpipes, and the swallows that
return here every year to nest, for Harry gathers up leftover
scraps at St Mungo's kitchens and feeds them to the birds.
Harry is a wiry little man, with battered, knobbly features,
and thick, strong hands, from a lifetime working as a
ship's stoker. When other homeless men take Harry for a
drink, they call him 'Grandad', but Harry has never
married. He has no children. And he has never had a
home of his own. Harry is 72, and came to St Mungo
fourteen years ago when Charing Cross first opened its
doors.*

I buried my mother in 1975. Until then I had always gone
back to Springburn, which was where we lived in Glasgow. I
had been at sea all my life, but after she died I went a couple
of trips and then gave it up. Something came over me. There
were plenty of relations, but no family, so I came down here
and stayed at a seamen's mission in Canning Town. They
gave me a nice room, and I found work as a porter.

I'd never married. Seen enough of that in my travels.
Always happy-go-lucky, that was me. Twelve years in the
Navy, serving on armed merchant cruisers and the aircraft
carrier HMS *Empress*, and then nearly thirty years as a
merchant seaman. Always a stoker. They were all coal-
burners when I started, but they'd turned to oil by the end. It
was hard work but I could handle it, because I'd helped my
father delivering coal. I was used to handling sacks of coal all
day. It didn't bother me. It was exciting at times, seeing
different places, different atmospheres. A quiet life, really. I
never got into any trouble, apart from this one night down in
Africa, right on the edge of the desert. I met this wee boy

from Glasgow who had joined the French Foreign Legion. He wouldn't tell me his name or where in Glasgow he'd come from, and he was running away from something. Said he wanted to marry this half-caste girl and took me to a café. Well, they called it a café but there were red lights outside the doors and lots of naughty girls. It was out of bounds to anyone from the Legion, and there we were, just sitting there at a table, when the door burst open and in came the Legion police with sten guns. This boy just stood to attention, and says, 'Keep quiet, Harry. Don't say nothing.' And that was the last I saw of him. They led him away, and I never saw him again. That was the last time I went to anywhere like that.

I've been to some good places, mind. On safari in Kenya and Fiji, going up into the hills with a guide and seeing the wild animals. You hear a rustle of leaves and it might be a lion or a tiger, and I've spent hours watching baboons.

It was a good life, really, I suppose. Only once did a ship go down under me and that was off the coast of Norway. A merchant ship carrying general cargo, she was, with a full crew of twenty-seven men. Ran into the rocks in a fjord, and down she went. God, it was cold. Right in the middle of winter. We took to the lifeboats. They picked us all up. No one was drowned.

I've seen plenty of action. When I was out in the Far East, on *Empress*, the skipper would invite us all up on deck to see these Japanese ships passing through the Malacca Straits. One time I was standing there and this kamikaze pilot dive-bombed us. We were all watching him as he dived down through the sky, bzzzzzzzzzooooom, CRASH, right into the side of the ship. Didn't sink us, but he left a big hole in the side.

Having always lived among men, I suppose that's why I came here, really. When I left the sea, I'd started drinking and then one night I was in The Chandos near Charing Cross and this fellow tells me about St Mungo. So I went down there. We slept twenty or thirty beds to a room at first, but that nay bothered me. I'd been used to that in the Navy, and then when the nurses moved out of the hostel next door I was given a room of my own and that was very nice. I've got my own room here, as well, and I've had my own window-box which gives me something to think about.

Harry Scroggie

Roy Smith

That's the thing I miss, really. Not having a garden. If I'd had a house I could have had a garden. If I had my life back over again I think I'd have stayed in New Zealand, found a little house there and a wee job with horses. I've always loved horses, ever since I used to work with my father. A horse to me is like a kiddie. They get to know your voice and your whistle – the birds are the same. They're always waiting for me. I've reared two myself. Fell out of their nests, so I took them back to my room and fed them from the kettle, and there's two birds out there now that are half-pigeon and half-seagull. That's something I've never seen before. One night I was sitting in my room reading a paper, when there came this tap at the window. It was one of the pigeons. He had missed me and so he came to find me. I opened the window and gave him some food. I'm grateful to St Mungo. They've given me somewhere to live. It's nice to have a room of your own.

An equally familiar figure in the West End of London is Roy Smith, otherwise known as Little Legs. He is a dwarf, standing 4 ft 2 in. tall in his stockinged feet, with a thick, burly build and strong muscular shoulders. Every day he works his pitches around Leicester Square, playing mouth organ, dancing, cracking gags or stripped off in all weathers to do his 'muscle routine'. He says, 'No one can do it but me. Being deformed I have big muscles but short biceps and they click. I can shake them all over, my muscles, and even make my belly move like a belly dancer.' Having been born with this deformity, Roy has made the best of it. At the age of 13 he was playing Bonzo the dog in a Richmond Theatre production of Babes in the Wood. *The audience would shriek with amazement when the dog suddenly jumped on its back feet and ran away! Roy was born to a Romany gypsy family. His mother was Jewish and he has taken her religion, although his conversation is smattered with Irish Catholic phrases. Theirs had been a Romany family for at least 200 years, travelling throughout Europe. He had four brothers and two sisters, and being the only dwarf says he became the 'pet of the*

*family'. They all moved to England when he was 2 years
old with their traditional creas (caravan), grais (horses)
and lurchers (mongrel dogs).* Roy has worked in circuses,
*theatres and other branches of the entertainment industry
all his life, turning to busking, spivving (selling bootleg
whisky and other dodgy gear) whenever he has had no
other work to do. He appeared in The Beatles' film*
Magical Mystery Tour, *has made promotional films with
Paul and Linda McCartney and Led Zeppelin; has
appeared in two films with Elizabeth Taylor (and many
other movies), and claims to have been the first man to take
a team of wrestling midgets on circus tours of the United
States and the Far East. He has also worked in variety
with stars like Vera Lynn and Wilson, Keppel and Betty.
He is now nearly 70, but likes to keep that fairly quiet, and
certainly does not look it, dressed in jeans, American
baseball shirt, denim waistcoat, silk scarf tied round his
neck, wearing a US Cavalry-style broad rimmed hat. He
carries a walking stick – not because he needs to, but
because it's a 'good worker' when he's doing a Charlie
Chaplin routine. Roy has often earned large sums of
money (but says he never counts it!), has been married
three times (always to tall girls), and has three children,
sons aged 41 and 17, who are both normally built, and a
daughter, Karen, 24, who is also a dwarf.*

Five years ago my Karen, she had a little boy. He lived three
and a half hours, God bless his soul. Her husband, black.
George. He's dead. Twelve weeks ago. Died of cancer. He was
like a diamond to her, but I was gonna kill him, you know
what I mean. She's small and had what you call a little chip
on her shoulder. She wanted a big black. I've been married
three times, and he was no bigger than me, you know what I
mean? The first wife, she was a singer. Good looking woman.
The next, 5 ft 11 in., champion ice skater. Met her in a
pantomime at the Empire Pool. *Snow White and the Seven
Dwarfs.* You can guess which part I was playing, but with my
drinking, it went the other way, know what I mean? She

went back to her mother, but then finds she's pregnant and my Karen comes along. Because my Karen is a dwarf, God bless her cotton socks, Trisha never accepts her. On my baby's life, on my Georgina's life (that's my granddaughter), I never tell a lie. Packs her in her carrycot, puts her in the motor. Six months old. That's what she was, and I took her back to my brother's and brought her up myself.

In 1964 I was down the Grave Maurice pub down the East End, waiting for the Kray twins. Good boys they were; I don't mind what people say. They was only bad to bad people, right? They thought the world of me. Called me 'The Kernel', right, 'cos I was like their court jester and Ronnie Kray was 'The Colonel'. I'm a bit of a character, right? Bit of a personality. I've done a bit of villainy in my time. It's all water under the bridge. I'm a good boy now, know what I mean? But I wasn't. How d'you think I got these broken knuckles ... last bit of bird I done was in 1976, and that was for doing someone with a knife, I didn't kill him. I was lucky, and now I'm ashamed of it. It was over business. This geezer wanted to work my pitch, and it got me upset. He hit me over the head, and then it was him or me, right? Another time I shot a geezer. I used to carry a gun in those days. Caught him with a nick at the side of his chest, under the armpit. Lucky again, thank God. I got four years for that. I've done a seven, a five, a four, a three, a twenty-one months, nine months and Borstal, but I am *not* proud of it, know what I mean? This geezer I shot welshed my father, God rest his soul. He was a street bookmaker. In them days you used to slip a bet, not like the betting shops you have now. This geezer welshed him for eighty quid, which was a lot of money.

You don't do things like that. Gotta be *straight* with people, know what I mean? I've had directors of factories come to me, want to buy cheap lighters – not cheap ones, but Calibri lighters, 'cheap', know what I mean? To give their *staff* crooked gear for Christmas! That's *wicked* ... I've done all that bent gear, razor blades, lighters, pens, always working the streets and that was how I first came to St Mungo's. I had this girl working with me. Alice. She's married now. Comes from East Acton. I asked her if she'd like to do the April showers, selling umbrellas, right? She says, 'Yes' and so I buys a gross of umbrellas at ninety-nine pence and she goes off down the Tower charging two and a half quid. She has a good day, comes back, and I says to my mate Chick, who's still here at St Mungo's, 'Can you fix us up tonight?' He lets us in the back door of Charing Cross, nice room, double bed, sweet as a nut.

Last time I had a place of my own was when I was with my wife. That was when I came out of prison in 1976. Then that finished, know what I mean? And I went out to the Far East – to Japan, Taiwan, Thailand, Burma and the Philippines with my act, Fuzzyball Kaye & Company. The ball was 'cos I do rollers. There was four of us, all dwarfs. We don't split the money. I pays them, 'cos I'm the guvnor, right? But on the way back I got ripped off in Djakarta and lost me money. Must have been over a grand, and so when I gets back to London I'm back to busking, and tossing the broads; that's what we call the Three Card Trick. The Queen's the lady, the broad. They never find her, know what I mean?

I was underneath the Arches then, for six or seven months, down the Embankment. I got a carrier, know what I mean? Two mates look after me sleeping bag during the day, and then if I've made enough busking, it's a bottle of Scotch for me, bottle of Martini for me mate, bottle of cider for this other guy, and some cigarettes. Every night I gets a taxi from outside the Tom Cribb pub down to the Apollo. One night this driver says, 'Where do you live, sir?' thinking I've got the flat above the fish shop.

'There,' I says, pointing to me sleeping bag, giving him a tip. He couldn't believe it, and goes back and tells me mates working the pitches in Leicester Square. Two of 'em comes down to the Arches, and Scotty says, 'Geddup' and brings me down here to St Mungo's. That was three years ago. I've been here ever since.

I don't blame me wife. How can I explain it to you? Owing to the drink, she couldn't suffer – and she's a good mother. I go down to see them all every week, two boys, one girl and me granddaughter, usually Sunday mornings, but I won't let them come up here to see me 'cos me youngest boy, he's 17, and he used to hang about the West End. Can't keep me eyes everywhere, not when I'm working, and he was disappearing into fruit machines. And the West End is dangerous. I'm ugly, but he's a good-looking boy, know what I mean? And you gotta worry about that, am I right or am I wrong?

Thomas Dillon is someone you might never notice, UNLESS you heard him speak. Short and slim, built like a jockey, slightly stooping, with a sharply defined nose and quick, darting eyes, he seems to be mentally running away while he's still sitting there, silk scarf loosely knotted around his neck; it's not until you look twice that you realise his trousers are torn, and the holes in his anorak have been roughly mended with a needle and thread. But Tom is one of the St Mungo success stories. A homeless man who came in off the street, whose problems were thought to be hopeless, and has now confounded everyone by settling down into a one-bedroomed Camden council flat, looking after himself, shopping carefully, and cooking casseroles and stew for himself, 'always putting in some garlic and some peppers . . . I like Indian and Chinese food, but it's expensive outside, so I use my own initiative. Don't throw away the end of the bacon; put it into the pot, with mince, onions and tinned tomatoes. They're from Italy, going up in price.' He is one of 400 men who have passed through St Mungo's into a place of their own, and he's looking after himself well – although he did cause a bit of a stir at the opening of the hostel in Tufnell Park by telling the Deputy Mayor of Islington that his name was Yogi Bear. It is when he starts to speak that you realise Tom is different. His voice has that soft, Dublin lilt. Sentences trail off in the air. His fingers hang suspended, and when he makes his point (which he does with all the skill of an artist), magical, sing-song, whimsical phrases somehow tack themselves onto the end of what he is saying; words that he has heard on radio or television, and which he will sing, whistle or hum, or deliver with a hiss or a hoot.

Now I had a little bet on this particular rugby team. The Irish team, that was fatal, der dum, der dum, der dum. I knooooOOOw! And then one of these guys, supposed to be an All Black from New Zealand, says 'Tom. TOM. TOM! Get a few bob on that, and you'll be all right!' – and, of course, they lose. Watching the game I was, the score was 9-9 at Lansdowne Road, woooo-wooo – and then just into injury time the Welsh drop a penalty goal, Shirley Bassey territory, Tom Jones, der dum, der dum, der dum, *It's Not Unusual*, der dum, der dum, der dum.

Right now, sssssshhhh. What did you want? Me a gambling man? Sometimes I am. And sometimes I am *NOT!* It all depends on the currency, or my, er, er, financial situation. Before I came up to The Establishment today I was watching a little thing on television, a series set in Scotland, about the bookies. I listen to the radio a lot, and I say to myself, now where shall I go today? Now, there's the Ideal Home Exhibition. It must be £4.50 to get in there – or there's the Museum of Mankind, and you can walk all round *THERE* without it costing a penny. This is no exaggeration, I tell you, no exaggeration. There are things there that they have brought from Indonesia, shrines, and things like that. So I said, why not venture up there and have a look-see. When did I first venture into St Mungo? Oh, George, GEORGE! Now let me see – that was in nineteen seventy ... seventy ... EIGHT. In the Charing Cross, right across the road from THE HOTEL.

I came in because I was, to a certain extent, destitute. Well, I wasn't destitute, but I had no money and nowhere to go. I'd had a little living-in job, outside Oxford, working in a hotel kitchen, and I packed that in. I did everything. Cucumbers. Spud-peeling. Cheese. You use your initiative in jobs like that, even though I'm not a professional. I've done a lot of work like that, but only on the casual. I took a job once, a regular job – and at the end of the week they give me this pay packet, and there were all these deductions, and I say to myself, George, what does this MEAN? Taxing me this and taxing me that. What the hell have I got here? So I go back to the casual, because then I know what I've got in my hand. So before I came down here to The Establishment this morning,

George, I went into this bar down the road and had a stout and barley wine. Mixed them together. Not too bad. It's all mahogany down there.

I was here for a long time, well, in this other establishment. They've knocked it all down now. When that closed I came down here to a single room, which I was very much fortunate to get when it first opened, and then later to Tufnell Park. Beautiful accommodation up there. My own room. Oh yes, oh yes, George. Magnificent. Had my own room, and could fry my own grub, but if you wanted to go down to breakfast, they would cook your breakfast. I have great admiration, and that's no exaggeration. They understand my problem, do you know what I mean, George? I'm not a very good conversationalist, but I have a problem, which they put down on paper – and here they understand me. It was a Dr Dracula and Mr Hyde sort of affair, you understand me, George? They would say, 'Oh well, boom, boom, boom,' – and they didn't turn me away, and seeing as it's Lent, at this particular time of the year, there's a lot of people from Ireland and Scotland, they could have turned me away, if you see what I mean. Sometimes, I'm very morbid but I like not to be.

I'm from Ireland myself, you know, between Dublin and Wicklow, out by the horse show ground, down by the river. My mother was a dancer with the Tiller Girls, and then later she used to do the Wall of Death, riding on a motorcycle. My father was a civil servant, but I didn't see him very often. They were separated; not like it is nowadays, divorced. I didn't leave Ireland. I just ventured away. Looking back on me now, I'm what? Born in 1936, what does that make me? Fifty-two this year. There we are now, der dum, der dum, der dum, Yogi Bear, yabba dabba doo. You see, I've travelled. This is really what it's all about. I didn't have any education, really, when you come to look back, and you ask yourself, why couldn't I learn *this*, or why couldn't I learn *that*? I can write beautiful. I can even draw, tsssscherooo, but I had very bad trouble with my *reading* and all that, and so, in other words, I got my education from *the outside*. Now, I only had two pints – a good combination. I call them a winter-warmer here, in this time of year, no *REALLY*, to tell the truth, whether I went away or whether I came back – that is the question. I used to be in the Merchant Navy, and in the good days when the docks were full up. There was more ships than men, in the fifties, sixties and early seventies, and then the whole thing turned around. Some people saw the writing on the wall. I was an able seaman on the deck, decks and cranes. Us people, the seamen, never got pensions. They'd just pay us off at the end of a trip ... they went off to Australia, New Zealand, America and Canada, and I should have done that, George. Look at the change in Aussie now? You used to get all the people going out there for £10, some of them fell by the wayside, but some achieved great feats. It's a great life. I worked on the coal boats between Dublin and Liverpool back and forth, back and forth, and then the banana boats out to the West Indies; Jambelaya-come-bega Tambega Montego Bay, and then the passenger boats, down to the Cape and over to the Americas, then the lamb from New Zealand. It wasn't like it is now. There were no containers. Boy, did I like the girls – I've got a daughter in New Zealand. She's 28 now, and I've never seen her ... I was on the beach in Saigon. Went there with a tanker flying the Dutch flag, and I could hear the bombs falling – 55,000 dead, lot of them college educated, and here am I, no education – but not an imbecile, you know what I mean, George. Know what I mean? Perhaps I should have stayed there when I jumped ship, in Quebec and Seattle, but it's all there, George, in the Museum of Mankind.

Now it's all turned around. I got paid off, and then one morning I woke up and my papers had been stolen, my bag had gone, my discharge book, and they'd taken my shoes. I'd lost my identity ... and now it all goes by plane. The big bird, wooooooo, woooo. The big bird has taken over, George. Flying taxis. And now when I go back to Ireland, all the theatres have been knocked down. It's all gone. I was brought up on pink sheets, blue sheets, and hot water bottles, not the rubber ones – but the other ones shaped like that drink from Holland, Bols. You can go into the second-hand markets now and see them. The cobble-stones have all gone now, George. You see, when I was a youngster I used to stutter, stutatatat, but I could always sing like a lark, George; always singing away like a lark, I was, all day long ...

Thomas Dillon

Carl Herde

Seeing him walk down the street, tall and erect in military-style raincoat, close-cropped and proud in bearing, no one would ever think that Carl Herde was homeless, but he is – because he chooses to be. Having twice lost all his money, Carl decided not to attempt another comeback. Realising that he was now poor, he chose to adjust his life accordingly, walked into Charing Cross, and asked for a bed. That night he slept in a dormitory with thirty other men. There was the usual smell of unwashed bodies and feet and stale clothing. Nevertheless, Carl decided to stay, and over the years that followed started to explain his background. Carl is a former officer in the German Army who fought against Britain in the Second World War. Under Common Market legislation, he has a right to live wherever he chooses in Europe – and he prefers London. His homelessness does not cost the British taxpayer a penny. Carl, now 72, receives a pension from the German Government and pays all his bills personally. His room at Lancaster Road is always immaculate. Carl is tidy and correct. His manners are precise, and the staff of St Mungo's say that he has a leavening effect on every house he stays in. Anyone visiting Carl would find him sitting squarely at a table, back upright, hands either side of a book, moving occasionally to turn a page. This is how he spends his days, but not all of them. This is Carl Herde's story.

I am, of course, perhaps, not typical of the people you look for. My past is quite different from most people, but here I am saving money. I am living on a small pension from Germany because I lost twice all my money, and when I was about to start for the third time I thought it wasn't worthwhile, so I came here. I had to sue the German Government five times to get all my benefits. I was victorious on four, but lost one. In Germany it is very easy to sue the Government because it doesn't cost you a penny, except for your lawyer, and my best friend is a lawyer.

The first time I lost my money was because I gave a bank guarantee to a very good friend for half a million marks, and he went bankrupt. I had to pay up and that was all I had. That's about £200,000. That was in 1965, and in my disappointment I went to Chile in South America and started in a glass factory, which I already knew from some friends there, and then I went through two or three revolutions and four presidents. I was caught in a restaurant with some very good friends. They were very enthusiastic about this latest revolution, and I said to them:

> These militarists are no more bearable than anybody else. Perhaps they may be worse. Don't expect anything better because they have gained power by revolution ... when they have the power they will start to kill people and intimidate people just like the rest.

That was in 1973 when Pinochet had just taken over. At the next table there was a relative of a colonel. He heard what I said and they arrested me, put me in prison, and, of course, that made my business impossible. It wasn't a very big business, about 180 people, but in Chile that's a lot, and in the end the German consul got me out of prison, and took me into the embassy for six months. In the meantime, the consul negotiated with the Government and I was received by the Interior Minister.

The Minister said, 'I have looked at your file and I can see that there have been mistakes on both sides,' which I could not agree with, because the only mistake that I had made was to say what I thought. He said, 'If you will declare now, in front of me, without putting anything in writing, that you regret what you have said, then it will all be over.'

I said, 'Minister, I was drunk when I said it, but now I am sober and the more I think about it, the more I think that I was right when I said it.' That, of course, was the end of the interview. The consul was livid with fury, and I was thrown out of the country. I went back to Hamburg, which had been my home city, but by then I had been away ten years and didn't understand the people any more. They were no longer speaking my language. All these trendy words, and the attitude – they seemed unfriendly. On the trains I didn't know what the fare was. I looked around and realised that I didn't feel at home, and so I sat down and said to myself, 'Where have you been happy in your life?' And that was London. The very best friend that I have ever had was Admiral Cowland, although he died soon after I came here. He was an engineer and also harbour-master in Alexandria after the war. I met him there when I was working as a representative for a very famous English firm, Napier, which was then a daughter firm of English Electric, now General Electric, selling turbo-blowers. He was the chief engineer for the company that I was dealing with, and we became very good friends. In the war, we had been on opposite sides.

I was in a crack division, the First Panzer Division, and fought in Poland, briefly, and then in France and Russia, three times wounded and thirteen times decorated. Iron Cross Second Class, Iron Cross Third Class, and then for certain attacks. I am a potential war criminal according to some of your newspapers, but you will find that no officer or man of the First Panzer Division has ever been accused of any war crime, as far as I know, and I think I know a lot. I look back on it now as a period of good comradeship and, quite contrary to what is now the trendy opinion, we were a Corps of very high spirits, very good spirits, and very good behaviour. Nowadays, you have only a very one-sided idea of how the German soldier behaved, and that is the idea of the victors. I speak frankly, you know. When I left I was a Captain. I was not really a tank man, but artillery, and for most of the war I was a forward observer, giving shooting commands from the Front. We always said that the Panzer-men had four centimetres of steel between their chests and the enemy, and I had only my shirt.

When I first came here in the fifties, as a German ex-Captain, I was very favourably received. The people from Napier's were all ex-officers. There is a certain cameraderie among soldiers of different sides.

Then when I came again, I had no money. The Government would not pay me because I had been away so long. They had to check everything against their records, so I started my law cases. Meanwhile, the only money I had was the gratitude of the Fatherland for my war injuries. A small pension because I was shot through the wrist and my hand is stiff. I had another shot through my knee, which was very grave but has turned out marvellously, and another by the side of my chest. I came here on 1 April 1976 to stay for three weeks with Admiral Cowland, but he died immediately, and so then I stayed for three months, then a year, and my money ran out. I had only the 300 marks a month, but, of course, I knew I would win my law cases, but these things take time. In the end they gave me back all the arrears, conscientiously. I didn't want to ask my friends for money, and somebody told me about St Mungo's at Charing Cross. It was awful, absolutely awful – these great wards for twenty or thirty men, and all you had was a bed. No one ever stole anything. We made the best we could, but it was awful. But I said to myself, 'You are now poor, so you have to adapt to the situation in which you are in. You have to be realistic.' So I did. After three years, I got my first pension and the arrears, and then applied for a room of my own.

I have liked it always in England. The people leave you alone. Nobody asks, 'What are you doing now?' or 'What are you going to do tomorrow?' And I like that, because I like to be left alone. I am always very busy. Originally, I was studying Buddhism. That was another reason I came to London, to find some of the material available here. I think I have read everything that is available in the English language on Buddhism. I speak and read well English, German and Spanish; I do speak French quite well, but with some difficulty. At the moment I am studying Germanic ancient history, about 2,000 years ago. I buy the books in Germany. Every spring I go to see my son in Hamburg – he is 41 and has been on a dialysis machine now for seventeen years. Last year he had a transplant, and it is very important to me that I see him every year, sometimes for four weeks, sometimes longer, and then in the autumn, every year, I go to Spain, to a little place called Trujillo in central Spain, between Madrid and the Portuguese border. A very small town of 8,000 inhabitants. I go back there every year and stay at the same small hotel. Trujillo was the birthplace of Pizarro, who conquered Peru, and also of Cortez of Mexico; many of the conquerors came from that small area around Trujillo, the poorest area then and now of Spain. Nobody goes there now, but me. There are no tourists, but I have a lot of friends there. I could stay with friends, but prefer to stay in this very cheap hotel. I prefer my independence.

Now I have lived with St Mungo's for about eleven years. They are all friendly, and I have had some of my best experiences here. I like the English people. I know Charles Fraser and, to a certain extent, Mr Lane, and Ann (Lusk). Everyone has been very good to me, and I am not the type to ask for help. You see, I do not believe in God in the Christian sense. I do not believe in an after-life or, in the Buddhist sense, in the life-after-life, but I do believe that moral standards are, to a certain extent, rewarded, even if you are disappointed many times. I am leading an intellectual life. I could, of course, have a flat, and it might even be cheaper, but that would increase my responsibilities. I do occupy relatively little space which, in reality, could be occupied by somebody else, but this is the way it is. I started with St Mungo's, and am very much the kind of person who stays, just as I always go back to the same hotel in Trujillo, or, if I go to Madrid, always return to the same place. I have a happy life and am even, to a certain extent, optimistic, although I see things as they are and have no illusions. When I left school in 1933, conditions were very bad in Germany, and although my mother and father did everything they could to help me I couldn't go to university. Now, I am educated, although it is purely for my own enjoyment and pleasure. It helps nobody but me when I study the history of the Goths, but what can you do in life? You have a good meal and it gives you a certain pleasure. With me, it is the same with a good book.

Similarly, no one would suspect that Charles Chitolie had been homeless. He is 30 years old, lean and fit, trendily dressed in a washed blue denim suit and sneakers, eyes bright and open-gazed. Charles was born in St Lucia in the West Indies, and came to Britain when he was 9. His mother is in London, staying with his brother's family in Hackney. His father is in St Lucia. For the last eight years Charles has worked for a firm in Hendon measuring fluids

*for automatic filling machines. He has never been out of
work, but three years ago he found himself homeless with
the beginnings of a drink problem.*

It was getting divorced that started it all. We had bought our
own property, but when we decided to get divorced in 1985
my wife and I both realised that neither of us could afford to
keep on the flat. We had been married about seven years and
were buying this co-ownership flat down Ladbroke Grove,
near the Tube station. It was costing us over £300 a month,
which was OK with our combined salaries, but more than
either of us could manage on our own. I still see my ex-wife
quite often because we have a son, Ashley, and I go down to
see him almost every weekend, and sometimes during the
week, picking him up from school. He is 6 now.

The marriage went wrong because we had financial difficulties at one time. This led to arguments and we went off
each other. We started to think we weren't suited to each
other. We talked about it and realised that the best thing to
do was separate and get divorced. We thought it was no good
making each other unhappy when we might meet someone
else with whom we could be happy. My wife was working for
a housing association, and it was she who first heard about St
Mungo. She telephoned them and found about these flats in
the Cromwell Road.

I never went through really bad times. I didn't have to
sleep rough. I went straight from Ladbroke Grove to this flat
at Cromwell Road, which I shared with two other blokes. To
be honest, I didn't like that very much. One of them had been
through a divorce as well and had been badly affected by it.
His wife had gone off with someone else, and he'd really hit
rock bottom. I never found out why the other chap was there.
Thursdays was the worst. That was the day the Social Security money came through and all the blokes went off drinking.
Some Thursdays I used to sleep on the sofa at work, covering
myself with curtains, because I didn't want to get involved in
all that. I went through a spell of drinking myself, around
the time of the divorce, blaming myself, and all that, and
then I'd go round and bang on my wife's door, which are the
sort of silly things you do . . . being with St Mungo's helped

Charles Chitolie

Charles Hamilton

me sort myself out. I was able to talk about my problems and put my name down for a bedsit or a flat. After five or six months they moved me to a single room in Lancaster Road which was much better. That was in 1986, and I stayed there another three or four months before they helped me get a flat from the Royal Borough of Kensington and Chelsea. I don't think I'd have been able to get one if it hadn't been for St Mungo, because they helped me when I was ready for it and had sorted myself out. I was only drinking because I was lonely, and gave that up after a while, because there are other things in life. I'll always be grateful to St Mungo's because they gave me another chance. Really, I don't think I could have done it on my own. Now, I've got a girlfriend and see her once or twice during the week, and at weekends we often take my son out together, the three of us, down into the country.

Another person whom one might never think had been homeless, and truly desperate, is Charles Hamilton, an Old Etonian from a wealthy family of bankers and lawyers. His father was a manager for the Westminster Bank. Charles is still a St Mungo's resident with his own room at Bravington Road. Charles has been with St Mungo for five years, initially as a resident at Endell Street. After a severe mental breakdown, Charles' financial affairs were put under the control of the Court of Protection. The Court has control over his assets, paying his rent direct and giving him a twice-weekly allowance for food and other living expenses. His most serious problem is drink. Charles has a large beer belly and is of medium build. When we met on a day in March that was not notably sunny, he was wearing a straw hat with the silken band of the MCC, a City-style blue-striped shirt, open at the neck and bursting at the buttons, an expensive-looking tweed jacket, casual trousers, a battered pair of shoes — and no socks. His voice was rich and fruity; his complexion puffy. Periodically, his cheek muscles twitched. This is his story.

I don't know why my family sent me to Eton. Perhaps my mother thought it might be good for prestige. I spent five years there, from 1957 to 1962. Jonathan Aitken was there with me and Lord Soames' son, Nicholas Soames. He's now in Parliament, too, I believe. Don't know what all the rest are up to. Most of my friends seem to have ended up in the City as stockbrokers. See them sometimes, but don't go to the Old Boys' Dinner. It wasn't the happiest time of my life. Fagging, and all that nonsense. I was fagging for Lord Stonor, who is now the Earl of Camoys. He's got a big house down near Oxford.

I worked regularly until about 1974, and then as a culmination of heavy drinking and slight money problems I had a certain amount of mental and psychiatric trouble, I was in a psychiatric hospital, had to sell my properties, and lived in a bedsit for a little bit. In 1980 and 1981 I ended up with the Salvation Army, which was absolutely terrible, and then I was put in touch with here by the probation officer at Bow Street. I'd been picked up drunk and disorderly in the Covent Garden area; a few times, quite close together. The magistrate thought I needed help. I don't know what was turning me to drink. Boredom, I suppose, and the psychiatric problem I had. Manic depression. I've been all right for the last three years, since I've been at Bravington Road.

I think it was stress at work that triggered off my illness. When I left Eton I went into the Stock Exchange as a brokers' clerk, a Blue Button, doing all the running around for the broker, checking prices and all that business, ringing the prices back to the office. If I'd stayed there I could have been a broker by now. I was also in the wine trade once. Should have stuck at that, learning the business. Then I could have become a buyer and a Master of Wine. Not a bad job, that. I enjoy drinking wine, but it's hard to afford these days. Boozing is damned expensive. There's a bit of Italian stuff around, and Greek wine. That's not *too* bad.

I'm a beer drinker now. Five pints a day, mostly. Can't afford spirits, unless I have a bottle indoors, sometimes. Drank twelve pints a day when I was working in a warehouse, children's and men's wear, sorting, unloading, getting off orders to the branches. I've done all sorts of jobs. I was a porter at Marsham Court when Francis Pym was living there. Terrible job, that. Flat porters are not the nicest people. Bitchy sort of people. Never told him I'd been to Eton, too. He would have had a shock if I'd told him. He was Defence Secretary at the time. That was 1979–80. Haven't had a regular job since then, just kitchen portering, that sort of thing. Twenty quid in your hand for a night's work. Not bad, really, I suppose for ten hours' work. Cash in hand, no questions asked. There were always casual jobs here. Washing dishes, peeling potatoes, mopping floors. Sometimes, I'd prepare food but not very often.

I've been quite lucky with money, really. I've never lost much. Made a bit of money on shares now and then. Made a bit on unit trusts and gilt edged. I've always been careful, but in 1975 when I went into hospital the psychiatrist heard I had money and thought it would be a good idea if I came under the Court of Protection. They look after my money now. I can't touch the capital. I go in twice a week. £40 on Monday. £40 on Friday. I suppose it's a good idea, but I was never really bad with money, even when I was ill – apart from once when I started selling off furniture that I'd inherited to buy drink. That was when the psychiatrist intervened. I did once have an expensive holiday. Went to Sicily after seeing *The Godfather*, stayed in a big hotel for a fortnight, caught the train to Rome and then flew to Ibiza and stayed with my parents there. But that's the only time I've done anything silly.

I have never married. Can't afford it. Quite enough problems of my own without having to worry about a wife and children. I don't think I'm emotionally mature enough to get married. The thing about St Mungo's is they give you a roof over your head. They've given me a nice bedsit, sharing the lounge and kitchen. Eight of us live there. There's been quite a few changes. People come and go. You can have company if you want it, but not if you don't. It's fairly comfortable. They try to encourage you to move on, but not too desperately. I think I'll try to find a flat next year if I can.

I tend to get up fairly late, have a breakfast, and then you can guess what happens at eleven o'clock. I'm in the pub for a couple of hours in the morning; lunch here, indoors; have a small sleep in the afternoon, usually about two or three hours, and then go to the pub and have about the same again. Go to bed around tenish and read for an hour. I've read quite a bit of Jeffrey Archer recently. I like his stuff, *Kane and Abel* and *The Prodigal Daughter*.

I've been pretty impressed by these people, since the probation officer sent me down here. The food's not too bad. It went down for a bit, but seems better today. When I was here they used to give you quite a good dinner for a pound. I still see my mother. She's got a nice villa in Portugal. Before that she was in Ibiza for twenty years. I have been there quite a few times. Hope to go to Portugal again this year.

Just one look at the features of Joe 'Packy' McParland tells you his trade. That broken nose and the two bright pink cauliflower ears. Now, at the age of 75, Joe is a little unsteady on his feet, but still knows how to roll with a punch – and if he has a night on the beer (which is not unknown), the staff at Endell Street have to handle Joe with a certain amount of care. Once a boxer has learned how to deliver a punch, the knowledge stays – and Joe quickly squares up to anyone who upsets him (and he gets upset on the beer, sometimes). Joe was brought up in Dublin. His brother Jack and three sisters still live there, but they are married. His 'family' is now St Mungo's. Although he talks of 'going home to Dublin', no one thinks he ever will because Joe has been saying that for twenty years. He keeps himself clean and well dressed, but his memories are all set sixty years ago, in the days when he was a professional boxer.

It was a hard game when I was in it. Always fifteen rounds. I went to the top too quickly. That was my trouble. I was a bantam-weight. Became famous overnight. Took a feller's place one night down at the Primaland in the East End. That started it. I was a substitute job. All the fighters used to go down there. Kid Lewis and Kid Berg came out of there. It was always a hot spot. 'Who'll fight Connie Lewis for six quid?' the geezer said. 'I will,' says I. I was an overnight sensation. They went wild. That was the Thursday night. Sunday night was the big night. I boxed three times in ten days once. It was a hard game. Terrible. 'McParland's Third in Ten Days', it said in the paper. Headline news it was. Terrible. Should never have been allowed. Madness. I was only a kid of 18, but I liked the applause. They used to make a fuss of me, following me around the streets, asking for my autograph.

I beat Dickie Corbett, and he went on to become Champion of England. We had two fights down at the Hoxton Baths. The first was a draw. The second, I beat him on points. He finished up in the Bethnal Green Tube disaster, poor fellow.

If I had my life back over, I wouldn't do it again. Boxing's dangerous. I blinded a darkie one night. He went blind in the ring. I'd hit him once and was just about to hit him again, and he says, 'I'm blind . . . I can't see.' This was a return fight. He got the first one on points. Kid Shepherd his name was. The papers said 'Lucky Kid', when they wrote him up. Terrible, terrible. Don't know what happened to him. Dickie Corbett's brother lost his sight in the ring, as well. Another headline was 'Irishman's Chivalry'. I wasn't Irish. Not at all. The old man scarpered when the First World War broke out; he wasn't having any of that.

I should have made a fortune, but I never kept it. Fifty quid a night was all I used to get in those days, fighting at the National Sporting Club. The most I ever got was 200 quid for a fight in Belfast, and my Dad hung on to the money. I was always sending money home as a kid, twenties and thirties out of every fifty, and they had no need of it. The family were bookmakers. I was born in St Helens, Lancashire, where the Beecham's Pills come from, in 1913, and then reared in Dublin. Went to the big infant school and had a good schooling. My Dad had a big book in Dublin, and made a lot of money out of the game; lived in a big house with chauffeur-driven cars, and owned two or three beauty parlours. He hired an aeroplane once to go to a Meeting. The Flying Bookie. He used to put on some shows. Where we lived was a rough centre and I was always fighting on the streets. I liked it when I was a kid, but I took a lot of beatings in the end. I was lucky, though. Never had a cut around the eyes; never lost blood. I used to train at Dyer's Gym. A few big fighters trained there. Fred Dyer's long dead, and his gym is now part of a foreign embassy in Agar Street, opposite the old Charing Cross Hospital.

Jesus, it's terrible what I've done with money. I should have gone to Australia, which was what they wanted me to do after I beat Dickie Corbett, but I would have spent it all. And I worked so hard for it. Up every morning doing road-work to keep the legs right. Always fifteen rounds; had to keep your legs right.

I spent ten years in the fight game, but didn't hang around after I'd finished. Worked with the Electricity Board in Dublin and here in London, laying cables. I've lived in lots of places, but always in rooms. I've never had a place of my own, and never lived with a woman. I had a place in Camden Town for a long time. This landlady wanted me to move in with her, and then my mate came in with me. He moved in with her instead.

I was going with this one woman in Dublin for two or three years. She went off to Edinburgh, and I went after her. Brought her to a party at our house one night, and she couldn't get the drink down quickly enough. My old man says, 'I'd leave her alone.' The only girlfriend I'd ever had, she was. The one and only.

Now I spend my days looking for a Samaritan, but they all seem to side-step me.

Lastly, there is John. That is not his real name. Alone among those interviewed, he asked not be identified (for reasons that will be understood). John is another St Mungo success story. He is 35 years old, and has been homeless for about fifteen years, until he arrived at St Mungo's in August 1985 straight from a Buddhist mon-astery, with his head shaved. Throughout those years he had drifted from job to job, always restless, sometimes staying in bedsits or with friends, and living for four years in a dosshouse. His longest period of employment was eighteen months in a lard factory, first as a cleaner and then later as a storeman. Now, for the first time in his life,

Joe McPartland

'John'

he has a small flat with a London housing association, found by St Mungo's, and has re-established contact with his family.

My problems started with all the moving about we did when I was a kid. My father was in the RAF and we kept moving from town to town, and then to Cyprus. We were quite a large family. I had two brothers and two sisters. When he retired we all went down to Devon. He became a pig farmer. The trouble was I could never got on with him, from the time I was about 13. He'd want me to help him with the pigs and I'd always refuse and there'd be great arguments. Sometimes he'd send me to my room, and he used to beat me quite a lot.

I left school at 16 without any O-levels, which is one of my great regrets, and soon after that went into the Army. My father was dead against that, but thought about it overnight and then next day said perhaps it would make a man of me. So I went off and joined the Royal Corps of Transport, hoping to become a driver. That was a great mistake. I couldn't handle it. They sent me up to York to take a physical education course because I needed building up, but when it came to the Passing Out I always seemed to be the one that dropped out.

The Army wasn't what I thought it would be. I had seen all those films in which they tell you about the comradeship, but it was never like that for me. I just wasn't the ideal soldier. It was not in my nature. I was untidy, wore those John Lennon-type glasses, and could never keep myself clean. My uniform always looked terrible. My trousers always seemed baggy.

In the end, I tried to buy myself out. I think I was homesick, but that cost £250 in those days and my parents couldn't do it. They didn't say they wouldn't; they just *couldn't* do it, and so I cut my wrists with a razor, which is a criminal offence in the Army. They locked me up in the guardhouse and took away my tie, my belt and my shoelaces so that I couldn't try to commit suicide again, and gave me an escort wherever I went, cleaning out the barracks. Then I was bummed out and sent home. I was 17 then. My father disowned me the following year. I'd rather not say why. Personal reasons.

For a few weeks I worked with a travelling fair, rolling my sleeping bag down in the back of the lorry in which they carried all their gear. I did all kinds of jobs. Worked in a toy factory, a cash and carry, an engineering firm, and all sorts of other jobs. My longest job was in a lard factory down in Rotherhithe. I did that job for eighteen months, cleaning the floors and then becoming a storeman, living then in a doss-house in Deptford. I stayed there for four years. At first I had a cubicle, which was about 6 ft by 4 ft, and then later they gave you a 'special', which was about twice as big with its own key. I also went through a sort of late-hippie phase, wearing Afghan coats with my hair all long.

For the last eight years I've been unemployed. It's getting harder and harder to find work. I've never felt settled, and I think it's all that travelling I did as a kid that started it. I just can't seem to find a job that I like.

About four years ago I read this book about Buddhism that had a photograph of a monastery down in Sussex. I wrote to them and this monk invited me to go down. At first I went for the weekend, then stayed ten days, and they invited me to become an anagarika, which is a trainee monk. You shave your head and dress in white. I thought it was paradise at first, but it was hard, getting up between five and six in the morning to do meditation, and then doing my chores and other work. For a while they made me head gardener and I also worked in the forest. (The monks had their own forest about a mile from the house) – but I was hyperactive, I couldn't settle down, and kept fidgeting through the meditations, which didn't go down too well.

I was there about eight months, and then this monk that I'd liked was promoted and sent to a monastery in New Zealand, and this new teacher, or bhanti, arrived. He was an American ex-marine. With him it was back to the old Army days, making life difficult, being very strict. It wasn't a happy ship to be on any more, and I was in the process of leaving there when this other trainee told me about St Mungo's. I arrived here with my head shaven, but they didn't seem to mind. They took me in. That was in August 1985.

At first I stayed in Endell Street, and then in the November they offered me a room in Bravington Road which was the first place I'd had of my own. That's when I started getting a few possessions together, and then after about a year and a half they found me this flat I'm in now, which has a bedroom, living room, kitchen and bath. The DHSS gave me a grant to buy some furniture, and I started getting a few things around me. I've got a television, a home computer (mostly to play games, although I've also tried making up my own programs), quite a collection of books about chess and Tibet, and, most important of all to me, a telephone. That keeps me in touch with my family and friends.

When I was at Endell Street, I phoned my sister one day, quite by chance, and she told me that my father had just died. I hadn't been in touch with them at all for about sixteen years, but I had kept saying to myself that the time had come when I should try. There were many times when I wished I could have put right what was wrong, but I kept blaming myself, which I think was the reason I kept trying to commit suicide. I tried at least a dozen times, overdosed, tried to poison myself with white spirit, and tried to hang myself. And then I did and he'd died, which shocked me quite badly because I'd learned to forgive him while I was in the monastery and I was ready to see him. Now, I've got in touch with my mother again and I can go down there to see her whenever I want to. She keeps me in touch with all the family gossip. I don't need anybody to live with me, and I've no intention of getting married. I love my own way too much. I can like it or lump it, although when I feel really down it's good to know the 'phone is there. I haven't tried to commit suicide again in recent years.

I think St Mungo's has given me back my confidence and my self-respect, and now this past nine months I've been studying night classes, taking a course in book-keeping. Once I've taken the first exams, I'm going on to take a course in technical accountancy. Ideally, I'd like a full-time job, but whenever I go for interviews they tell me I'm too old . . .

Chapter 10

So now you have met them, The Homeless – ordinary people, much like you, but perhaps more reluctant to accept responsibility (because they may have lived institutionalised lives), more nonconformist than society permits, possessed of an ingrained and incurable individuality for which the State makes few allowances. Men, for this is a book largely concerned with men, who have chosen to steer well clear of love, family, work, taxes or friendships, which are the normal framework within which the rest of us live our lives; and who may have reasons for their decisions that they would rather not explain.

It is a strange indictment of our society that no one knows how many homeless there are. Estimates of the numbers of homeless people on the streets of London alone range from 6–8,000 to as many as 30,000, though the latter figure appears unlikely unless one includes (as many campaigning organisations would) those who are clinging to some form of basic shelter, like the large hostels provided by the Salvation Army and Church Army Housing, and the seamen's missions which still exist in the East End of London, and the more squalid bed spaces available at the lower end of the bed and breakfast market. If one includes all these together with the large numbers of homeless families now accommodated in grubby hotels by local councils and the DHSS, then even that figure of 30,000 becomes an underestimate, and one probably approaches a figure of around 100,000, living in wretched conditions in the otherwise prosperous city of London, although Brian Boylan would tell you that there are worse conditions than these to be found in the slum quarters of Manila. But is this how far our values have deteriorated? Has the quality of social judgement in Mrs

Thatcher's Britain so deteriorated that one has to compare our inner city problems with those of the Philippines or Calcutta? Must we conclude that Mother Theresa was right in drawing parallels between the conditions she saw on the streets of London in April 1988 with those that exist in the Third World? Has Britain, or its Government, ceased to care?

Whatever the statistical truth (and I have been careful throughout not to use figures that cannot be substantiated), the hard fact remains that you can miss a late night train and walk through the streets of London and find fellow human beings, mainly men, many of them young and apparently fit (although there is a high percentage of mental illness among the homeless), sleeping in back street doorways, off Piccadilly, Oxford Street, Regent Street, Charing Cross, Tottenham Court Road and the Strand, beneath the Arches, along the Embankment, stretched out on benches in the London parks, around Parliament Hill Fields, and all around the main line railway stations – and you only have to walk around these areas once to realise that there are many thousands of them. Their condition attracts an occasional speech in the House of Commons; the Press become interested if a Mother Theresa spends a night amongst them; the *London Standard* periodically publishes an article that reads much like the last; the television documentaries now fall into a predictable pattern – and most politicians steer well clear of this subject, for they *know* that there are few votes to be won in pleading its cause. Their constituents are largely indifferent to the plight of the homeless. Charity fund-raisers find it far easier to raise money for cats and dogs than they do for projects providing accommodation or assistance for the homeless, with the result that many charities themselves lead a hand to mouth existence, sometimes having to devote as much energy to their own survival as to the people they wish to help. The man in the street, with a wife, a mortgage and

children to feed, instinctively senses that many of those
who are homeless need not be; that they are not society's
rejects, but all too often men who have themselves
rejected society's norms. He has to make a thousand
minor adjustments to get through life, so why shouldn't
they? His indifference is hardened by the suspicion that
the homeless themselves rarely show gratitide; many of
them really will tell you to 'Bugger off!' if you offer them
anything more than what they want, which may just be
fifty pence for a cup of tea, or a watertight pair of boots,
and unless you can find the resources within you to meet
them face to face as St Mungo does, never moralising,
never sermonising, and never trying to do more for any
man than he really wants to do for himself, there may be
nothing you can do.

This may be part of the reason for St Mungo's success.
It has adopted a management style and an ethos that is
totally different from that of any other homelessness
charity. St Mungo neither campaigns nor engages in
party political debate and consciously avoids religiosity,
although many of its staff are drawn to this work through
a sense of commitment and caring that owes much to
their personal beliefs. There is now a clear divide
between staff and residents. The staff are paid wages for
their work, observe hours and conditions like anyone else
in employment elsewhere within the State, and are
encouraged to regard their work as *work*. 'I think one of
John Lane's great contributions to St Mungo is that he
has developed further this principle that the residents
pay *rent*, and that there is then a contract between them
and the staff. They pay that rent, and then get their
accommodation, breakfast every day, other meals if they
choose to pay for them, and are otherwise left to lead their
own lives,' says Boylan, adding that this is a mature
management principle and one that works.

At the same time, there remains a gentle pressure on
those who are able to settle back within the community

to do so – and with that a realisation that some of the homeless men are drawn to St Mungo because there may be some other problem in their lives that makes it extremely difficult, if not impossible, for them ever to be able to live in a self-contained dwelling of their own. Some St Mungo residents have grown old without ever learning to fend for themselves.

One has to accept that many of these men are selfish. 'They are very ungracious and ungrateful,' says Mick Carroll.

There was a worker in Endell Street, a Dutch woman who had trained as a social worker in Holland, came over to work here to broaden her horizons, and finally went back because she said she had given *everything* she had and got absolutely nothing back. She had enjoyed the stories, and sustained herself, and enjoyed the crack, but she got nothing back from any of these guys. They would have walked over her sooner than help her out with a problem.

We had one guy who died in his room and his room-mate didn't tell us he was dead until twelve hours later. This guy just sat there reading his paper, went for his breakfast, returned to his room, sat there reading again, then went for his lunch, and we might not have known for days that this guy had died if someone hadn't asked where his key was. His mate says, 'He won't be needing it now . . . he's dead!'

Residents here are often hard and selfish. You have to grow into caring for others, past all the difficulties you have in being cared for by other people – some of these guys never seem to have grown past the stage of being fed like birds. That's what a lot of the guys are stuck with. They have got their beaks open, and they haven't got the mechanism to close them again and start looking for their own food. And some of them never will solve their problems because they've been burned out by drink, sorrow or disappointment.

It says much for the staff of St Mungo's, and the way they are led, that they can recognise and live with the defects that many of their residents have, accepting that thieving, violence, drunkenness, dependency on drugs or alcohol, mental illnesses or physical disabilities are no more than the facts of some people's lives, and those who happen to possess them may nevertheless be deserving of kindness.

However much one qualifies this judgement, there remains something quite remarkable about St Mungo and the way it has quietly grown over the past twenty years from a man with a pram serving soup to the homeless to a large complex of hostels and houses, with a staff of nearly eighty (including caretakers, cleaners, cooks and maintenance men), providing good quality accommodation every night for over 500 homeless men, many, as we have seen, with serious mental, physical or behavioural problems. All this is done within an annual budget of £1.8m. The Housing Corporation and government departments have helped with funds and mortgages, but only after being shocked into action by two freebooting pioneers, Paddy O'Connor and Jim Horne, and the embarrassing furore that surrounded *Goodbye Longfellow Road*. Had all this happened in the slums of Calcutta, on the streets of Soweto or among the downtrodden poor of Palermo, one suspects that there might have been more public sympathy, both for them, and also for those whom they were trying to help.

Now, there are more homeless people than ever on the streets of London. A decade of severe unemployment has taken its toll, with our prisons full to overflowing and homeless men from Britain's poorer regions taking refuge in the anonymity of London's streets, and growing evidence of homelessness among the racial minorities – and all within a few hundred yards of Downing Street, Whitehall, Parliament and the City of London.

The Government's policies have made matters worse for the more deprived members of society. Changes in Housing Benefit and the DHSS rules regarding the payment of various forms of social security have all added to the problems of homelessness. Britain, which already sends more of its citizens to prison than any other Western society, is responding to the social tensions that are now accumulating within by toughening its laws and building more gaols. Housing conditions in the inner city, where homelessness is concentrated, continue to deteriorate, with even those authorities which have willingly carried out the Government's policy of selling council houses being denied the right to use the proceeds to improve their housing stock. Those authorities like the Greater London Council and the metropolitan councils which sought to tackle homelessness on a city-wide basis have been abolished by the Government, and little has been done to replace them.

Because the poor are always with us, is that any reason why society or the Government should be so reluctant to help them, and so unwilling to make adequate funds available for their accommodation? Can we all be indifferent to the fact that there are groups of homeless men like those to be found on London's streets gathered in the centres of all Britain's major cities – Birmingham, Glasgow, Edinburgh, Manchester, Liverpool, Leeds and even Swansea, Gloucester and Plymouth? Do we have to wait until each one does something silly, like stealing a bottle of milk or urinating in a public place, before providing them with accommodation in gaol? Do we have to wait until their mental condition deteriorates so far that they can only be kept in a large institution? Quite apart from any wider social considerations – or those of plain decency – lies another simple fact. Britain is wasting enormous sums of public money keeping men and women in prisons and mental institutions when they could so easily be looked after better and at less cost, shown kindness and given more personal freedom, in places like St Mungo's. Within the financial resources made available to it (and these only made available through fear of further scandal in the field of single homelessness), St

Mungo's has built up its small chain of hostels and bedsit properties in just five years. Half the budgetary cost comes from Government through various forms of Housing Grant; the other half from individual residents, usually through the income received each week from the DHSS. Without St Mungo's, many of them would either be on the streets, in prison or in mental institutions. If they were in prison, they would each be costing you, as a taxpayer, £12,700 a year[1] to maintain. If they were in mental institutions, they would be costing nearly £18,000 a year.[2] But St Mungo is able to produce beds for the homeless for less than £5,000 per person per year, including in that figure all its running costs and overheads (averaged out), and also the costs of its resettlement work and work experience services.

Of course, there is a price to be paid. Society has to realise that homeless men may be nearing the end of a harsh life that has left them strong-willed, bloody-minded or cantankerous; that they may only be helped if not on their precise terms then through an acceptance that there is no such being as the 'typical' homeless person, that each individual has to be treated with respect and an acknowledgement that the best work in this field is often done by those who are difficult, tough or gutsy themselves, and maybe even a little eccentric.

John Lane lays down only three basic rules in the hostels that now come under his overall management:

1. No resident may interfere with another's privacy;
2. No violence (anyone who is gets thrown out on their ear); and
3. Pay your rent.

In addition, John Lane and his Committee have defined

[1, 2] These were the current figures at the time of writing. The figures are updated annually, and are taken from Answers to Parliamentary Questions reported in *Hansard*.

a Statement of Purpose, within which all St Mungo's future work and developments will fit (see Appendix C), including shelter for all who need it, asylum for those who are so vulnerable that ordinary hostels are insufficient, training for residents who desire it, leading, hopefully, in the end to some of them finding full-time employment, or even starting up on their own. Residents are now encouraged to participate fully in the day to day running of their hostels as part of the preparation for leading independent lives.

Any casual visitor to St Mungo's hostels would find the atmosphere relaxed, because these simple rules, sensibly applied, provide tight boundaries within which each establishment is run. Provided a resident observes them (and he must pay his rent), he is free to come and go as he pleases, although he will soon become aware that there is a gentle pressure being exerted upon him to take more and more responsibility for his own affairs, until he reaches the point (if he can) where he is able to live on his own, with only minimal support from St Mungo's.

'These boundaries are very important,' says Lane.

I have tried my utmost to prevent St Mungo's becoming a bureaucracy, although we all face the danger of being sucked into the system now that we are organised as we are, and receiving what are, for us, large sums of public money. The other important thing that we have to retain is our street credibility; we have to keep the trust of these guys, and we can't continue to do that if we become too formal. I have been to the United States and seen the large hostels run by voluntary agencies in Boston, Washington and New York, where you may find as many as 2,000 people living in one building, sleeping forty beds to a room. There is nothing quite as bad as that in this country, although we have to remember that America started emptying its mental institutions long before we did, and now has this massive problem of 30,000 homeless people wandering the streets of New York, and tens of thousands more in other cities, preponderantly black, like the population of our prisons. The danger signs are there for us to see.

What I think we have proved at St Mungo's is that there is scope for the hostel with eighty or a hundred beds, and that this can be part of a resettlement process within the community *that works* provided the boundaries are clear. Living in a hostel is like being a child in a family (and there is a *real* parallel). A hostel has to provide the stable living regime within which the individual feels safe and able to grow. We would like to open more hostels and expand our programme, helping more homeless people to resettle back into society, but at the same time we recognise our own boundaries. You can't have a massively bureaucratic organisation and still relate to those who are housed within it. But it is possible to open hostels like ours and still maintain street credibility. I think we have proved that, too.

Appendix A

Letter from Mrs Barbara Castle, Secretary of State at the Department of Health and Social Security, detailing the basis on which the GLC could make use of the Charing Cross Hospital building.

DEPARTMENT OF HEALTH
AND SOCIAL SECURITY
ALEXANDER FLEMING HOUSE
ELEPHANT AND CASTLE LONDON
SE1 6BY

TELEPHONE 01-407 5522

PO(H) 1807/7   26 April 1974

Alderman L O'Connor
Greater London Council
Members' Lobby
The County Hall
LONDON
SE1 7PB

Dear Alderman O'Connor,

You wrote to me on 25 and 27 March about Charing Cross
Hospital.

I do appreciate how anxious you are to use part of the building
to accommodate homeless single people as soon as possible. For
my part I wish to cooperate fully with you and your Council,
but I must safeguard the interest of the NHS staff who must
continue to occupy part of the building for some months.
Having seen the account of the on-site meeting of officers on 26
March, I am ready, pending the drawing up of a formal licence
to occupy and use the premises, to grant entry to the building
as soon as I receive a letter from the Greater London Council
accepting the conditions set out below. It must be understood
that while this will allow Council officials to enter the building
to plan and to undertake works of maintenance and adaptation,
no single homeless are to be allowed to move in until plans
have been agreed and carried out to seal off the Health Authority accommodation and to provide the necessary fire safety
facilities for the NHS staff who are to live there. I do not think
this need give great difficulty or take long to be completed.

The conditions for the licence are as follows:

1. The GLC to occupy and use the building for a period of six months certain, thereafter terminable upon the giving by my Department of six months' notice to vacate the premises.

2. The GLC to pay a nominal sum only for the use of the building.

3. The Health Authorities to continue to occupy and use an agreed area of the building (the area to be determined between the Health Authorities and the GLC) without payment except as specified later in this letter, for as long as needed.

4. The GLC to undertake all necessary repairs and maintenance to the building, to prevent deterioration having regard to the fact that it is listed as being of special architectural or historic interest.

5. The GLC to provide heating, electricity and water to the area occupied by the Health Authorities, and to pay the rates and other outgoings of the Hospital building.

6. The Health Authorities to pay a proportion, related to use, of the costs incurred at items 4 and 5.

7. The Health Authorities or the Crown Estates Commissioners or other respective agents, to be allowed reasonable access to the building in pursuance of action for the ultimate disposal of the property.

8. The area occupied by the Health Authority's staff to be afforded privacy by sealing off the area in so far as this is consistent with safety requirements.

9. The accommodation will be generally maintained as a hostel to which men are accepted on referral from recognised agencies and not as an overnight shelter. A charge will normally be made for residence.

In addition to the above conditions, the Council will need to examine the safety aspects, especially fire risk and adequate escape provisions. You have previously mentioned the requirement to notify the Westminster City Council of the intended change of use and will no doubt ensure that the new use of the building satisfies Westminster's public health requirements. We have to face the fact that the cost of keeping the building open is considerable but I agree that it could well be less than the £2,000 per week mentioned, since this figure is related to hospital use. But in any case Health Authorities will contribute a proportion of the running costs while their staff remain in the building.

I look forward to receiving your comments on this letter which I have copied to Westminster City Council in case they wish to raise any points affecting, for example, public health and social services. I hope that you will now feel more content with the possible costs of the project. I look forward to seeing you later.

Yours sincerely,
Barbara Castle

Appendix B

The report signed by the GLC Director General (Sir James Swaffield), the Comptroller of Financial Services (Maurice Stonefrost) and the Controller of Housing (Harry Simpson) on 22 March 1977. Appendices B and C have been omitted since these were merely lists of properties.

Greater London Council

Housing Development
Committee

Report (22.3.77) by

Director-General
Comptroller of Financial
Services
Controller of Housing

Item	
3	Hg.140
SHORT LIFE HOUSING PROPERTIES ALLOCATED BY THE HOUSING DEVELOPMENT COMMITTEE SINGLE HOMELESS SUB COMMITTEE	

Summary – This report reviews the work of the Single Homeless Sub Committee and in particular its relationship with two specific organisations featured in the Yorkshire Television documentary programme 'Goodbye Longfellow Road' shown on 8 March 1977.

1. Introduction

1.1 The Committee, at its meeting on 3 March 1977 considered a confidential report (Hg 81) which examined the Council's working relationships with Housing Associations and voluntary bodies with particular reference to those allocated short-life properties. Of this latter group the main attention was focussed on those properties allocated by the Single Homeless Sub Committee.

1.2 The report recommended improved procedures and tighter control over the various organisations and it was agreed:

(a) That all housing associations, charities or other organisations holding, or to be granted, GLC short life properties on licence, be informed forthwith that for the retention of existing, or the grant of any further GLC properties, the minimum accounting and administrative standards (outlined in the report) must be complied with;

(b) That in the event of non-compliance in respect of any of these conditions, all the properties be withdrawn from the association/organisation concerned;

(c) That a further report on the additional staffing and/or means of redeployment necessary to achieve (a) and (b) above be submitted as soon as possible.

1.3 Since then the Yorkshire TV programme 'Goodbye Longfellow Road' has been screened and aroused a great deal of public interest.

2. 'Goodbye Longfellow Road'

2.1 In the officers' view no attempt was made in the TV programme to examine the homeless problem as a whole and it was clearly aimed at spotlighting what was alleged to be 'profiteering from human misery'. No mention was made of the Council's significant achievement in providing shelter for many hundreds of unfortunate people who would otherwise be on the streets and for whom little if any provision is made in either the public or private sector.

2.2 The film was heralded as a 'major documentary' and will no doubt be rated highly in terms of television research and reporting. It depended heavily for its impact on revealing 'facts' and situations calculated to shock the average viewer and undoubtedly succeeded in this respect.

2.3 However, in doing so, some events were portrayed in an unnecessarily unfavourable light, (e.g. that it was necessary to move home in an open lorry) and similarly statements were made which, had they been checked with the Council in advance, would have been found to be incorrect, e.g. alleged payments in respect of a non existent house. Little attempt was made to provide a balanced report. There was no mention of several offers of rehousing which were made to one of those families concerned or of the payment available towards removal expenses or of home loss payments.

2.4 In order to present a more balanced picture a brief resume of the Council's activities in the field of housing for the single homeless would seem to be necessary.

2.5 Some of the main issues raised and questions posed in the programme are set out in Appendix A together with factual information which will enable these matters to be assessed in a balanced context.

3. Single Homeless Sub Committee

3.1 Early in 1974 the plight of the single homeless had become a matter of increasing concern and officers were under pressure from Members to identify Council owned property that might be made available to voluntary organisations on a short life basis. It was decided that help for the single homeless should be channelled through the St Mungo Trust Charity with whom all negotiations for the grant of premises should be conducted. Three properties owned by the Council had been made available to the St Mungo Trust Charity, these were:

(i) The former Marmite Factory in Durham Street, Lambeth;

(ii) 39–43 Battersea High Street, Wandsworth;

(iii) Lennox Buildings, Vauxhall Cross, Lambeth.

In all three cases, the Trust was occupying the buildings free of charge but accepted responsibility for all other outgoings. The report, Hg 199, explained that the old Charing Cross Hospital would shortly be made available for accommodating the single homeless, and following consideration of the report, it was agreed that a special Sub Committee of the Housing Development Committee should be set up to coordinate the allocations, etc. The constitution and terms of reference were as follows:

Constitution – Chairman and Vice-Chairman of the Housing Development Committee (ex-officio) and four other members, one of whom shall be nominated by the Housing Management Committee. (It will not be essential for all these members to be members of the Council.)

Order of reference – To deal, so far as the Council has powers and within financial provision in the estimates of the housing programme group, with the use of short-life property not otherwise required for family accommodation.

3.2 By May 1974 Charing Cross Hospital became available and it was proposed that the Council should grant a licence to the St Mungo Trust for the use of this building as a centre from which people would be referred to other short life properties to be made available by the Council to approved organisations. A report dated 1 May 1974 by the Director-General to the Single

Homeless Sub Committee recommended that the sum of
£100,000 be made available to be expended by the Sub Committee for repairs, heating and lighting, etc., on the premises
allocated to St Mungo. This became known as the Charing
Cross Project.

3.3 A considerable amount of time and effort was spent on the
Project and over 500 bed spaces have been made available in
the Charing Cross Hospital, Lennox Buildings and the
Marmite Factory, and these continue to be well utilised. The
total expenditure to date by the Council on the three buildings
is as follows:

(i) The Old Charing Cross
    Hospital   – £13,728.49
(ii) Lennox Building   – £48,491.19
(iii) Marmite Factory   – £ 1,194.87

                £63,414.55   (A further £3,233.62
                                  is due making
                                  £66,648.17)

3.4 It was originally intended that the £100,000 budget of the
Housing Development (Single Homeless) Sub Committee
should be expended solely on the Charing Cross Project
managed by St Mungo but this was extended by a report dated
17 March 1975 to include NOVO on the grounds that this
organisation accepted referrals from Charing Cross.
Subsequently (report dated 24.7.75) it was agreed that the
budget be devoted to 'Single Homeless Projects' (generally)
rather than the Charing Cross Project alone.

3.5 The original £100,000 provision was virtually exhausted by
the end of the 1975/76 financial year, the unspent balance
having been brought forward from 1974/75. A further £50,000
was, therefore, allocated for 1976/77 (Report Hg 793 25.3.76).
Current expenditure (as at 28.2.77) has reached £141,069.32
over the three years and has been allocated as follows:

Organisation	Date of 1st Payment		Total Amounts	Notes
			£	
Annie Besant	29.4.76		450.00	
Bow Mission	24.7.75		8392.15	
Calix Society	27.8.75		2853.40	
Middlesex H.A.	5.3.76		4200.00	
NOVO	17.3.75		40238.34	
Prisoners' Wives	5.9.75		281.46	
	June 1974		13728.49	Old Charing Hospita
St Mungo Community	June 1974	£63414.55	48491.19	Lennox Buil
	17.10.74		1194.87	Old Marmit
Simon Community	March 1976		2000.00	
*Second Genesis	15.10.75		19239.42	
			£141,069.32	

*Note: Properties transferred to NOVO in November 1976.

4. Scale of the Single Homeless Operation

4.1 Apart from the three properties comprised in the Charing Cross Project, between 80 and 90 individual properties have been made available to a number of organisations dealing with single homeless. Although it is not possible to be exact in the matter it is estimated that between 700 and 800 people nightly have thereby been given shelter as a direct result of the Single Homeless Sub Committee's actions.

4.2 The number of individual properties is gradually declining as they are either required for demolition or, in a few cases, rehabilitation, and the position as at 28 February 1977 was as follows:

Annie Besant House	1	
Bow Mission	3	x Not within the
Calix Society	1	purview of the
x Cameron Group	1	Single Homeless
∅ Legion of Mary	1	Sub Committee
∅ Let Live	2	
∅ Melting Pot	1	∅ No payments made
Middlesex Housing Association	7	
∅ NACRO (National Association for the Care and Resettlement of Offenders)	3	
NOVO	46	
x Penrose Charities	1	
St Mungo Community (Not including Charing Cross Project)	7	
TOTAL	74	

In addition, St Georges Hostel, Millman Street, Chelsea is allocated to Simon Community and 14 Richmond Avenue, N1 is occupied by 'Prisoners' Wives' but it is now required for inclusion in the 1977/78 programme for the rehabilitation of acquired property.

4.3 This figure must be seen against a further 1703 short life properties currently on licence to Housing Associations, etc., which do not come within the purview of the Sub Committee. It actually comprises 4% of the total.

5. Second Genesis

5.1 This organisation first appeared on the scene on 23 September 1975 when it 'took over' 73 Alma Road, SW18. Instructions were received from the Chairman of the Single Homeless Sub Committee on 6 October to transfer 16 Vauxhall Grove, SW8, from NOVO to Second Genesis and a further property, 6 Sylvester Road, E8, was allocated in the same manner on 6 January 1976.

On 3 February a number of properties in the Belhaven Street area of Tower Hamlets were allocated to Second Genesis by the Chairman of the Single Homeless Sub Committee as an emergency measure to forestall expected squatting. The Renewals Branch of the Housing Department had no prior knowledge of the allocation and there was no opportunity for a proper professional survey of the properties. Indeed, had time been taken for this, the risks of squatting in this well organised area would have been very high. The properties in question were acquired under slum clearance procedure as part of the East London Open Space Complex and as such were technically unfit.

A further allocation, in similar circumstances, took place on 10 and 17 February.

5.2 In the fortnight between 3 and 17 February 1976, Second Genesis took over some 28 properties without prior inspection by surveyors from Renewals Branch. On 17 and 20 February Dangerous Structure Notices were served on eleven properties in Jupps Road including six occupied by Second Genesis and it therefore became necessary as a matter of urgency to allocate a few further properties to facilitate the re-housing of the occupants of those dwellings where Dangerous Structure Notices had been served. The final total of dwellings occupied by Second Genesis was 38 of which 28 were slum clearance properties.

5.3 Having regard to the very poor condition of the properties coupled with the need for speed and hence the unorthodox method of take over, it was quite impossible at the time to exert proper control. Works of an emergency nature were continuously being carried out, sometimes without prior agreement and always to a very low standard, so that R Branch with its limited resources was reduced for a time to checking, after the event, that claims for payment reflected reasonable value for money.

A list of properties together with details of payments made is attached as Appendix B.

It will be seen that apart from 16 Vauxhall Grove and 21/23 Grove Road which are both large properties capable of providing several units of accommodation, the individual amounts expended have been comparatively small and in the main have constituted no more than 'first aid' type repairs required to make the dwellings reasonably habitable, This is, in fact, what would be expected in respect of properties of the type allocated to Second Genesis. Wherever possible the works were agreed in advance and in all cases were inspected afterwards before payments were certified. It must be said, however, that the standard of documentation was not as comprehensive as would normally be the case for substantial works carried out in a normal manner, but in the circumstances, the officers attempted to strike a reasonable balance between what was desirable and what in the event was possible. It was in the light of experience gained in this respect, that proved not entirely satisfactory, that the recommendations in paragraph 1.2 above were brought to the Committee.

5.4 The period of time during which Second Genesis was active, i.e., October 1975 to February 1976, was so short that it was not possible to examine in sufficient depth the bona fides of the organisation although every effort was made to do so. Information as to rent levels they were charging and schedules of occupation were obtained in February 1976. Attempts continued to be made to regularise their method of operation, with little success. In October 1975 it was established that Second Genesis was registered as a company limited by guarantee. Although they declared an intention to register as a charity and a housing association, neither of these proposals came to fruition.

5.5 As early as January 1976 officers became concerned that all was not well and, after discussion with the Leader and the Chairman of the Housing Development Committee, the Leader ordered an officer investigation. At the same time, the Chairman of the Housing Development Committee instructed that no further properties should be allocated to Second Genesis. Following an attempt by both the Council's and the District Auditors to investigate the organisation the matter was reported to the Police and statements were made by officers but the matter was never finalised. In August the Director of Legal Services, on the instructions of the Leader of the Council, referred the matter to the Director of Public Prosecutions and investigations are still in progress.

6. National Organisation of Victims and Offenders (NOVO)

6.1 This organisation first became known to the GLC in 1973 when it applied to be accepted as a housing association to which the Council might provide financial assistance. The application revealed that NOVO was a registered charity and was also registered by the Registrar of Friendly Societies, under the model charitable rules of the National Federation of Housing Associations, as a housing association. The management committee of the association comprised an estate manager, a surgeon, a solicitor, a community relations officer, a hostel warden, a prison officer, a police officer and a member of Hackney Borough Council. All these were accepted as being responsible persons and the application was accepted in principle on 12 November 1973. For the avoidance of doubt, it should be made clear that the organisation was registered as a housing association under the Industrial and Provident Societies Act 1965 which at that time was the only form of registration required by the Council. NOVO has not to date achieved registration by the Housing Corporation under the Housing Act 1974, although the Council was informed by the Housing Corporation on 16 April 1975, that an application had been received. There were no dealings whatsoever with NOVO as a housing association nor was any financial assistance sought or provided by the Council for this purpose.

6.2 In May 1974 a letter was received from Hackney Borough Council which asked that numbers 136, 144, 146 and 148 Lansdowne Drive, E8, which were at that time being acquired by the GLC from the London Borough of Hackney as part of this Council's Broadway Market development, should be allocated to NOVO.

The first payment to NOVO in respect of work carried out at 136 Lansdowne Drive was made in March 1975 by which time a number of further properties had already been allocated to them. It should be stated that the type of properties licensed to NOVO are generally of a more substantial type than the slum clearance properties taken over by Second Genesis and were in the main properties eventually due for demolition as part of the roads and schools programmes. They were not slum clearance properties. A list of the properties together with details of payments made is attached as Appendix C.

It will be seen that the amounts expended on the NOVO properties are in some cases relatively large. This is due to the more substantial nature of the properties, the life span intended for them and the fact that many of them have been converted into hostel type accommodation. The works have been carried out to a reasonable standard, have been agreed in advance, inspected both during progress and after completion, and have generally been adequately documented.

6.3 It must be said that whilst NOVO have in the main performed in an acceptable manner as regards their relationships with the Council under the terms of the licence there has been trouble associated with their method of operation and this has led to Police Court action. As a result it was decided in September 1975 that no further properties should be allocated to NOVO and this has generally been the case although it has been considered reasonable on one or two occasions to allocate properties for specific reasons. Apart from the matter referred to in para 6.4 below, these amounted to only 4 properties.

6.4 Upon the collapse of Second Genesis in November 1976 it became necessary to consider urgently what should be done not only with the properties but more importantly with the people occupying them. The Council under the terms of the licence had no rehousing liability but when the organisation ceased to exist, it was not possible to ignore the situation whereby those persons living in Second Genesis houses would again be without accommodation. The only reasonable alternatives when Second Genesis became defunct overnight were for the Council to take over direct management or for the property to be transferred to another organisation. The former would have involved considerable management problems with likely pressure for immediate rehousing of all occupants, a liability which the Housing Management Committee would have found difficult to accept without detriment to many other urgent claimants. In the event, having particular regard to the very low standard of property, etc., it was found that only NOVO was willing and would be in a position to take over at least until alternative arrangements could be worked out. The report, Hg 16, dated 26.11.76, which the Committee approved sets out the problem and, in fact, mentions the temporary nature of the action taken. The breathing space obtained has been used to investigate the state of individual properties, the problems of the occupants, and the Council's capacity to deal with these insofar, for example, as rehousing is needed and justified. Six properties have been so far withdrawn and arrangements for a further nine are in hand.

6.5 Appendix A does not purport to be an exhaustive coverage of the many allegations and questions included in the TV film. It will take some time to check out every point but a start has been made to examine NOVO rents and to resurvey certain properties mentioned in the film in connection with alleged payments for work not carried out.

6.6 A further report will be submitted in due course when the investigations referred to in 6.5 above are completed.

6.7 The Committee will wish to know that in a Parliamentary reply on 14.3.77 the Attorney General said while speaking of NOVO that 'in the light of statements made in a recent TV programme and recent newspaper reports, I have now referred that matter also to the Director of Public Prosecutions'. The Council will welcome a thorough investigation.

Concurrent report (22.3.77) by The Solicitor and Parliamentary Officer.

Legal powers to make payments

In my opinion it is within the Council's powers to make available (either directly to proposed residents or to third parties who will make the properties available to proposed residents) property held for a function of the Council, until it is needed for the function, on licence or short tenancy, on the basis that it will contribute to the cost of repairs and maintenance. This arises in particular from the discretion given by S.111 of the Local Government Act 1972 which itself gives statutory expression to a long held principle of Common Law. In my view the Housing Act 1974 does not render unlawful such an arrangement with an unregistered housing association.

'GOODBYE LONGFELLOW ROAD'
COMMENTS ON SOME OF THE ISSUES RAISED IN THE
FILM

PART A

1. Opening Eviction Scene – This was an eviction of a tenant
from a GLC property on the grounds of serious rent arrears in
October 1976. As is customary, Tower Hamlets Homeless Families Unit and other social agencies were notified of the eviction
so that steps could be taken by the Social Services Department
to give the family shelter.

When the door opened the bailiffs were confronted with TV
camera crews. A Housing Department official was present and
was informed by a man who claimed he was a member of a
squatting group that he had arranged for the TV cameras to be
present. The tenant refused bed and breakfast accommodation
offered by the Borough and said she would return later to the
block as a squatter, but was advised not to do so. She left the
scene with what seemed to be a group of squatters.

2. Removal of Furniture from upper window into an open
lorry – It has not been possible to identify the address but the
impression given by the film was that the occupants were being
rehoused by the Council. The mode of transport used for remov-
als is entirely a matter for the person moving but where
persons are displaced the Council will pay reasonable removal
expenses.

3. The Thompson Family – Irene Thompson was a tenant of
Second Genesis at 30 Jupps Road and it is known that she
arrived homeless from Hull but neither this Council's Housing
Department nor the Social Services Department of the Borough
had any knowledge of her prior to the making of the film. The
first that this Council knew of her plight was on 15 October
1976 when the Director of Social Services of the London
Borough of Tower Hamlets wrote to the Assistant Director
'Renewals' advising him that Yorkshire Television were fea-
turing Mrs Thompson in a film and that she had been presented
to his office as homeless. The property was immediately inspec-

ted by a Renewals Branch surveyor who found that Mrs Thompson was not living in 30 Jupps Road and was, in fact, residing with her sister in number 17 Jupps Road (not a Second Genesis property). In view of the difficulties faced by Mrs Thompson and her two young children, immediate steps were taken by Renewals Branch to find another organisation using short-life property which would be prepared to accept the Thompson family. In the event, ACME Housing Association undertook to house her in a mobile home held on licence from this Council at 5 Camdenhurst St, E14 where it is understood she is now living quite happily. It is not the case that Tower Hamlets 'got the GLC to come up with the offer' as asserted in the film and the initiative was entirely taken by this Council through its short life operation. It was unfortunate that at the time when Mrs Thompson was due to move into the mobile home she had to enter hospital but the ACME Housing Association held the dwelling for her and she moved into it on her discharge from hospital.

4.   The Morter Family – The Morter's original private landlord would not agree terms for the property and it was not until the CPO became operative and the statutory notice of entry was served (on 12 February 1976) that the Council was able to assist in rehousing. The statement in the film that the Morters had had their bags packed since 1974 is therefore misleading. There had, however, been correspondence at Member level with the Morters prior to the Council acquiring the property and the Council's position was fully explained therein. Originally, the Morters stipulated a restricted area for rehousing but this was widened in June 1976 following further Member level correspondence. Between June and November 1976 the Morters were made 5 offers of accommodation and finally accepted one on 15 November 1976. Removal expenses have been paid: a Home Loss Payment has been processed by the Council and Miss Lillian Morter has been asked to provide letters of administration. Payment will be made as soon as these are received.

It is particularly difficult to understand why the Morters were depicted as moving at night and that they themselves were actually transported in the back of the moving van, which is normally not permitted by removal contractors due to insurance problems.

5.   Alleged Work on 23 Jupps Road – It was alleged that electrical work of a very poor standard had been carried out at this property and that payment was made based on 40 hours labour plus £45 materials for work that actually took half an hour. This property was not in fact licensed to Second Genesis and is squatted. The surveyor referred to in the film as visiting the property without having inspected the work was obviously not from the GLC.

6.   16 Vauxhall Grove, SW8 –The point was made that £4,800 has been spent on this property, that the drains and toilets are blocked, and that the tenants refused to pay rent. This is a large property and a fairly major improvement scheme to provide hostel type accommodation was carried out. The drains became blocked on a Friday afternoon in August 1976 but this did not prevent the occupants from continuing to use baths and toilets with the result that the rear yard was literally awash. The matter was discovered by a Renewals Branch surveyor on a routine visit and he immediately contacted Second Genesis and advised them to deal with the matter quickly either with their own builder or by calling in the Borough Council Emergency Service. In the event, the Borough Council call-out squad attended but were unable to clear the blockage and the matter was finally dealt with by Second Genesis.

7.   73 Alma Road, Wandsworth – It was alleged that after £728.83 had been paid on this property it was closed down by the local authority. The fact is that the local authority served two Public Health Notices on 30 May 1976 in respect of defective rainwater pipes, a sink waste, defective condition of the plaster in the first floor front room and the lack of one switch cover and a fuse box cover. The property has not been closed by the local authority at any time during its being held on licence by either Second Genesis or NOVO and it is currently being redecorated and the works stipulated in the statutory notices carried out.

8.   21/23 Grove Road – These are large four storey properties and were originally part of a terrace. They presented a good potential for conversion into at least 10 units of accommodation and as such a preliminary estimate was discussed with Second Genesis. As work commenced, Dangerous Structure proceed-

ings resulted in the adjoining properties in the terrace on which no money had been spent being demolished. It then became evident that whilst 21 and 23 Grove Road were in a better condition than the erstwhile adjoining properties it would be necessary to expend a larger than usual amount of money in order to prolong their useful life. Due to their size and form of occupation, it was also necessary to carry out fire prevention and means of escape work and this partly accounts for the level of expenditure being greater than customary on the type of property normally allocated to Second Genesis. Various alterations in the schedule of works were made and it was possible to reduce the estimated expenditure accordingly but the matter has been somewhat complicated due to the demise of Second Genesis during the course of the work. Further surveys are in hand to establish how much of the original work has in fact been satisfactorily completed and whether full payment has been made. There will no doubt be some further expenditure on these properties if the original scheme is to be carried through to completion.

9.   94 Dartmouth Park Hill – The film made some play of the fact that a payment had been made in respect of 93 Dartmouth Park Hill which quite correctly was shown to be non-existent. In fact, the payment was made in respect of 94 Dartmouth Park Hill and the confusion arose from a typing error in the report. All supporting documentary evidence carried the correct address.

10.   Frozen Food Centre – The freezer shop referred to in the film was 15 Bonnington Square, Vauxhall, which is an existing corner shop with residential accommodation over. It enjoys existing use rights as a shop and there is no reason as far as the Council is concerned why NOVO should not use the shop portion as a store for frozen foods in connection with their hostel operation. The officers are investigating the allegation that goods were on sale to the general public. The payment for repairs to this property were, however, in respect of the residential portion only.

Note – Other properties were specifically mentioned in the film but in the time available it has not yet been possible to examine the various allegations made. However, this is being done and a further report will be submitted.

PART B

At the end of the film several specific questions were asked and answers to these as far as it is possible to provide them are as follows:

a. Q.   Why has 89% of this financial year's funds of the Single Homeless Sub-Committee gone to just NOVO and Second Genesis?

A.   For the year ended 31 March 1977 £50,000 was allocated to the Single Homeless Sub Committee of which £30,047 has been paid for work carried out to properties allocated to Second Genesis and NOVO. This represents 78% of the total so far paid. It is obvious that as these two organisations have been allocated the bulk of the single homeless type property, they should have had the **highest** share of the payments. This is not without precedent as the number of organisations capable of dealing with this type of problem are limited and in fact during earlier years by far the largest proportion of payments were made to a single organisation, viz St Mungo. It must be stressed that these payments are basically on a once and for all basis in order to bring the property into a habitable condition. This, for example, is reflected in the case of St Mungo to whom very little has been paid since the initial setting up of the Charing Cross Project. It must be remembered as stated earlier in the report that substantial payments have been made on 1700 other short-life properties which are not within the terms of reference of the Single Homeless Sub Committee.

b. Q.   Why has NOVO now got 80% of the houses under licence from the same Sub Committee?

A.   As at 28 February 1977 out of a total of 74 properties, 46 were held by NOVO, that is 63% and not 80% as quoted in the question. The reason for this large proportion is covered in the previous question.

c. Q.   Why have large grants for housing single homeless gone
to properties, some unfit, one used for other purposes, some
demolished and one never existed at all?

A.

<u>Second Genesis</u>

The answers have already been given in the main body of the
report. The only large grants paid in single homeless properties were in respect of 16 Vauxhall Grove (£4861) and
21/23 Grove Road (£7000). The work undertaken at these
properties was necessary to comply with fire regulations and
in addition most of the rooms were decorated, essential
plumbing including new baths and basins were installed,
together with electrical work and roof repairs.

£7378 was spent on the remaining 31 properties with Second
Genesis, that is approximately £200 to £300 per property for
essential repairs.

<u>NOVO</u>

Grants to NOVO are considered modest having regard to the
size, condition, and life expectancy of the properties. This
and other points raised in the Question have been answered
elsewhere in the report and this Appendix.

d. Q.   Why are NOVO and Second Genesis allowed to charge
rents of £100 a week or more for houses given to them free by
the GLC?

A.   Under the terms of the licence to NOVO and Second
Genesis rents should be fixed at a level acceptable to the
local Rents Officer as a 'fair rent' for a comparable property.
A rent return from Second Genesis was requested from them
in February 1976; this return indicated that rents were
between £3 and £8 per week per property. NOVO were asked
for details of rents along with all other single homeless
housing organisations on 27 January 1977. To date no reply
has been received. Officers are therefore seeking to establish
the information by direct inspection.

e. Q.   Why have organisations that include men with serious
criminal records been the main recipients of GLC support for
single homeless?

A. As shown in the main report the check carried out by the Housing Department into the bona fides of organisations include the names and occupations of the committee members. The officers have no alternative but to accept these on their face value.

f. Q. Why did Alderman O'Connor and his assistant Ann Clark when they had been warned of conflicts of interest with Second Genesis, allow themselves to get into almost identical relationships with NOVO?

A. Alderman O'Connor and Ann Clark were members of both NOVO and Second Genesis and resigned from both organisations as follows:

Alderman O'Connor – 20 November 1975
Ann Clark   5 January 1976

g. Q. Why did the GLC let Second Genesis continue to claim houses and money when they had known for months there were serious deficiencies in their accounts?

A. On 17 February 1976 Chairman of Housing Development Committee instructed that no further properties were to be allocated to Second Genesis. On 8 March this was amended to allow allocation of properties on a replacement basis only, thus allowing persons displaced on demolition to be rehoused. After 21 May 1976 no properties whatsoever were allocated to Second Genesis. Where properties had been allocated it was considered that they should meet minimum and essential repairs.

h. Q. Are the DHSS satisfied that all their £14 a week vouchers have been properly used?

A. This is a matter for reply by DHSS.

i. Q. Why did O'Connor's Sub Committee meet so seldom and is it true that there were only two votes in its entire history?

A. In an operation of this kind, it is inevitable that Chairman's action must be the order of the day. Any action by a Chairman is minuted and the papers are available for inspection. Sufficient meetings of the Sub Committee were held to formalise the various courses of action and it is not considered that further meetings were necessary. No particular significance can be attached to the fact that only two votes were taken relating to the Sub Committee's work. It is not customary to take a formal vote if the members of a committee are in general agreement on the proposals before them. The minutes of the Sub Committee and of its parent committee, and of action taken on their behalf between meetings, are open to public inspection and as the programme illustrated use has been made of this facility.

Appendix C

The St Mungo Community Housing Association agreed this Statement of Purpose in May 1988, providing a policy framework within which it will expand its development programme.

ST MUNGO HOUSING
STATEMENT OF PURPOSE

PURPOSE

SMH EXISTS TO IMPROVE THE QUALITY OF LIFE FOR
HOMELESS, SINGLE ADULTS BY PROVIDING
ACCOMMODATION AND SUPPORT AND, WHERE POS-
SIBLE, INFLUENCING THEIR PROGRESS TOWARDS
GREATER SELF-SUFFICIENCY.

SCOPE

SMH carries out this purpose to the degree that our imagination, resources and operating environment will allow, and
irrespective of the age, sex or race of the homeless, single adult.

ACTIVITIES

SMH's activities are essentially supportive not directive. They
are undertaken to address the various and changing needs of
homeless, single adults in ways that are appropriate, practica-
ble and effective. We measure the success of our activities by
how they are valued by homeless, single adults.

Our activities cover four broad areas:
  (i) Providing a range of accommodation which satisfies – both
       in type and degree of support – the varying needs of
       homeless, single adults.
 (ii) Providing general support services which enable
       homeless, single adults to optimise their individual
       potential. As a minimum, these services include:

       — Welfare, which provides access to – and, where appro-
         priate, advocacy for – the help required by SMH
         residents to cope with personal, medical, psychiatric,
         welfare or financial difficulties;
       — Resettlement, which gives practical guidance and
         information to support SMH residents in their pro-
         gress towards more self-sufficient accommodation;

— <u>Employment training</u>, which helps SMH residents acquire the necessary experience and skills to be able to move into work outside SMH;
— <u>Social and recreational activities and facilities</u>, which relieve the drabness of homelessness and create a framework for the realisation of personal worth through the building of social and personal skills.

(iii) <u>Providing specialist accommodation and support for groups with special needs,</u> both directly and as an agency for other organisations. These special needs groups include the mentally ill, the elderly, and those residents needing a high degree of care. Wherever this is possible, practical and desirable separate accommodation and specialist services will be provided for these groups.

(iv) <u>Developing SMH resources and responses</u> to improve the quality of life for homeless, single adults. These include the development of staff and facilities; research; special initiatives; fund-raising and publicity activities.

Appendix D

The annual budget of St Mungo is now £1.8m. Income and expenditure broadly balance, and the following segment analysis shows how the money is allocated.

FINANCIAL REPORT

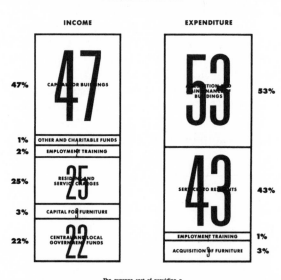

INCOME		EXPENDITURE	
47%	CAPITAL FOR BUILDINGS	ACQUISITION AND MAINTENANCE OF BUILDINGS	53%
1%	OTHER AND CHARITABLE FUNDS		
2%	EMPLOYMENT TRAINING		
25%	RESIDENT AND SERVICE CHARGES	SERVICE TO RESIDENTS	43%
3%	CAPITAL FOR FURNITURE	EMPLOYMENT TRAINING	1%
22%	CENTRAL AND LOCAL GOVERNMENT FUNDS	ACQUISITION OF FURNITURE	3%

The average cost of providing a hostel place for one week

Resident pays		Government pays				Care and welfare costs	Household costs	Maintenance
£41	+	£50	=		=	£33	+ £54	+ £4